Don't Kill Yourself
... Yet

Unleash THE SEVEN LIFE HACKS *to* *Crush Depression & Anxiety NOW*

Also by Michael McTeigue

The Keys to the Effortless Golf Swing
Curing Your Hit Impulse in Seven Simple Lessons
In paperback, e-book and audio editions

Bulletproof Putting in Five Easy Lessons
The Streamlined System for Weekend Golfers
In paperback, e-book and audio editions

Wild Times Ahead!
The Teen Girl's Guide to Guys, Sex, and Relationships
(Keenan Wilde, nom de plume)
In paperback and e-book editions

Don't Kill Yourself ... Yet

Unleash **THE SEVEN LIFE HACKS** *to* *Crush Depression & Anxiety NOW*

Michael McTeigue

Illustrations by Lawrence Moorcroft

To
Jane Roberts,
Carlos Castaneda,
Robert Monroe,
Bruce Moen,
and Ken Carey
wherever they may be…

Table of Contents

Acknowledgments

This book you're holding differs appreciably from the one I originally wrote. I shared my first final draft with a number of relatives and friends in hope of receiving useful constructive criticism, and—luckily for us—I did.

I'm deeply grateful to the following folks who read the manuscript carefully and returned insightful suggestions and abundant food for thought: Peter Mucha, Elisabeth Ostrow, my daughter Mindy McTeigue, Mary Banchero, Anthony Genovese, Gina Catania, Lauren O'Brien, Laurie Aames, and my cousin Kathleen McTeigue.

Special appreciation goes to my wife, Linda Jo McTeigue, for her ace editorial skills and more so for her acceptance and even encouragement of my eccentric notions about the human drama.

A huge shout-out to my talented and ingenious illustrator, Lawrence Moorcroft, who surpassed all expectations by bringing to life my cast of characters in a memorable and playful manner.

Do You Belong Here?

There are plenty of books about how to be happy, or at least happier... and this book is *not* one of them. If you feel "pretty OK" mentally, emotionally, and spiritually, and you want to nudge your well-being a little higher, you have seriously come to the wrong place. Likewise, if you're typically a cheerful person but a recent setback is making you unhappy—your lover cheated on you, a loved one died, or your house burned down—then you don't need this book, either. You will recover in time without *The Seven Life Hacks*.

On the other hand, if *relief from constant mental misery*—and clawing your way back up to "Neutral"—is all you dare to hope for, you *do* belong here. *The Seven Life Hacks* exists solely for readers who endure a persistent emotional state so awful that even a wisp of happiness feels permanently out of reach.

Tell me: Are you sometimes suicidal? Does your depression and/or anxiety haunt you with scenes of jumping off a tall building or fantasies of gazing down on your own funeral from high above? Have you considered filling your pockets with heavy rocks some moonless night and trudging resolutely from sandy shore into the deep, dark waters, never to return? Do you feel like the jaded, aging starlet filming yet another pathetic horror movie who wails, "Who do I have to *screw* to get *OUT* of this movie?"

If so, this book is my gift to you.

Don't kill yourself... not just yet, anyway. Instead, give *The Seven Life Hacks* a chance to help you emerge from your bottomless black pit and beat your depression/anxiety into absolute submission. You have suffered its domination long enough, and now it's your turn to dominate. After all, which do you really prefer being, the domina*ted* or the domina*tor*?

Choose *dominator*, and you will no longer feel like some sorry-ass, whipped, fearful, exhausted, devastated loser. You'll restore your life force, and in every conscious moment you will subtly vibrate with your unique power. You'll win emotional and mental freedom by implementing *The Seven Life Hacks* described in this little book. Yes, it will take some time to fully recover, but I believe you'll gain tangible relief very quickly.

How Can I Help You?

Resurrecting your life force requires focus, but it's not complicated. Hang with me, and you'll learn how four core issues annihilate your life force, moment to moment, every day: 1) your thoughts, 2) your interactions with others, 3) the circumstances of your daily grind, 4) your relationship with your body. I'll give you the hacks needed to halt the depletion *as it's occurring*. When you counteract these energies that enfeeble you, your life force automatically and miraculously starts to renew itself.

As a mega-bonus, we'll renew your life force *without any processing*. That's unique! There's no lengthy analysis of your inadequacies, mistakes, losses, or regrets. You don't ponder or process your "issues." You simply learn to neutralize attacks on your life force in real-time. You *can do* this!

Will you be truly happy? That's asking a lot! But you'll no longer be miserable; that is my commitment to you. I am confident *The Seven* will bring you relief because I developed and distilled these seven hacks through years of trial and error in battling my own depression.

Just A Few Words About Me

Originally, I was a cocky, unbridled optimist. While studying Psychology at UCLA, I adopted as my guiding principle this famous maxim attributed to Charles DuBois, "*The important thing is this: to be able at any moment to sacrifice what we are for what we could become.*" This single sentence plunked me on a zig-zag path after college to become TWA flight attendant, PGA golf professional, published author, member of the Screen Actors Guild, Stanford MBA, commercial real estate agent, serial entrepreneur in divergent industries, business consultant, and investment banker. At each juncture, I sacrificed whatever I had previously attained to undertake something completely different. In retrospect, this was downright foolhardy because continually starting new careers put me at a serious disadvantage to those with decades of *relevant* experience.

Even worse, starting in the 1980s, I enthusiastically endorsed the New Age proclamation that mankind was on the immediate verge of long-heralded enlightenment and revolution in human consciousness. Undoubtedly, I told myself, my true purpose for being here was to partake in this great spiritual transformation. I don't need to tell you how that's turned out!

And so, my unabashed optimism gradually deteriorated into dogged depression born of thwarted ambitions and dashed dreams. (For you movie buffs, I was as punch-drunk as Rocky after the 14th round!) This lasted more years than I care to recount. I used to gaze at the ledge out the window of my seventh-story office and wonder if taking the leap would bring blessed relief.

To pull myself out of the deep, dark hole, I tried talk therapy, medication, and workshops, and I read and listened to countless self-help books and audio programs. I ultimately succeeded in dispelling my depression and, along the way, developed *The Seven Life Hacks* system which I now offer to you.

I'm here with my hacks to handle the heavy lifting, to help blow away your persistent, pernicious distress and reboot your life force. *The Seven Life Hacks* will get you back to Neutral. Where you go from there is up to you.

How Miserable Are You?

By now, hopefully, all the well-adjusted folks have departed as instructed, and only true malcontents remain. To determine just how miserable you are, let's quickly assess your range of emotions during the past couple of years.

Look at the following diagrams. The horizontal axis along the bottom of each graph represents the past two years, with time moving from left to right. The vertical axis represents your mood at any given time, with the happiest you can imagine being at the top of the box, and your lowest, most miserable moods at the bottom. The line across the middle represents feeling Neutral—neither happy nor depressed.

The person in the following example was in a decent mood at the beginning, and then gradually fell into massive depression. S/he also showed more volatility in mood in the later months.

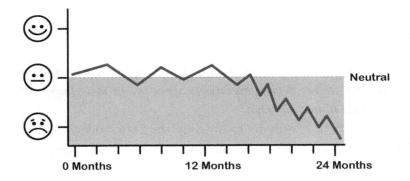

Grab a pen and draw a line across the page on the following graph, showing *your* typical emotional states as they have occurred over the last 24 months or so.

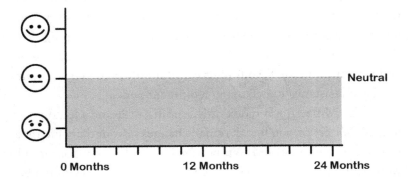

The area on the graph where you spend most of your time indicates your *emotional set point*, which is your most typical mood. Your personal set point these days lies well below Neutral, in the miserable region, does it not? As you make your way through *The Seven* and unleash the hacks in your daily life, your emotional set point will rise to Neutral or better and stay there. To achieve this, however, you must become a different person.

A Different You

First, ask yourself this: *am I truly willing to become a different person? Does my depression/anxiety serve me in some important way that I cannot abandon?*

Be honest with yourself. Close the book and take a few moments to ponder these questions: If you could beat your depression and anxiety into permanent submission by becoming a different person, would you do it? Starting today? If so, how far are you willing to go?

I assume you do not lack advice about how to improve your mental and emotional states. Your friends, family, loved ones, and therapists undoubtedly bombard you with suggestions and requests for new attitudes and behaviors. You resist, however. You are stuck where you are, partly because you resist changing. *The Seven* will help you—even drive you—to crush your depression and anxiety and restore your life force, but only if you release your stubborn resistance to becoming a different person.

How different? Paradoxically... both a little and a lot. As you unleash *The Seven*, you'll make small changes in your daily life that transform your mood and your personality in a big way. Your mind won't feel foggy and overmedicated—quite the contrary. You'll be more alert, more energetic, more engaged. You'll probably say, "I feel a lot better, like my old self... like my real self!"

Take ten seconds, right now, to really acknowledge your resistance. It is real, palpable, and perhaps the most substantial part of you. Answer honestly: ***How does your resistance to changing serve you?*** Can you abandon your "yeah, but" resistance, at least for a while?

Sorry, you cannot be half-hearted or half-assed about this. Either you commit to changing yourself in some meaningful way—which *The Seven* will help you do—or you stay stuck precisely where you are now. It is too soon to ask for hearty enthusiasm, so I will settle for your grim determination to be receptive to new ideas and try some new behaviors.

Can you picture yourself in a better state? Can you imagine a consistent feeling that right now, everything is "just fine"? Can you envision being centered, unflappable... *unfuckwithable*?

Don't screw with me or yourself on this. Go to a mirror right now and look yourself in the eyes. Make a firm, final decision. Do not continue to the next section of this book until you choose one of the two choices below.

☐   I will stay an enslaved, beaten loser. (Close the book. Bye Bye!)

☐   I will suppress my resistance to becoming a different person and use *The Seven* to restore my power and life force. (OK, please continue.)

Which Comes First?

As you well know, depression and anxiety contain both mental and physical aspects. Your mind is plagued with miserable thoughts and your body feels unbearably out of whack. *The Seven* addresses both dimensions, but which should come first?

Ideally, we'd hack your body first, giving you increased energy and stamina to tweak your mind persistently. That approach is unrealistic, however, because this book is for really miserable folks who can barely summon enough energy to read, let alone make sustainable changes in how they treat their bodies.

After careful consideration, I've decided we'll revamp your mind first, using simple but powerful hacks that will give you plenty of energy to restore your body. Let's get busy hacking your internal world!

PART ONE

Hacking Your Internal World

"You cannot have a positive life
and a negative mind."

Joyce Meyer

Welcome to the Shit Show

Who the Hell Are You, Anyway?

Before you can deploy *The Seven,* we need to establish exactly who you really are. This topic has confounded humans for centuries and spawned countless theories about the nature of human consciousness. But because your life force is so depleted, I won't waste your energy on an entertaining and educational *tour de force* of the many wild concepts endorsed by philosophers, theologians, healers, psychologists, scientists, and new age spiritualists since the dawn of human self-awareness. Such discourse would easily eat up a whole chapter, yet it will not relieve your misery for more than a few moments.

For our singular purpose—to resurrect your life force as quickly as possible—let's stick with what we know for sure: *you are the one who is miserable.* You have awareness, and you are painfully aware that you feel like crap, consistently and continuously, right? That miserable, crap-feeling entity is the one I am here to help.

How did you get this way? Perhaps you believe you are miserable because of the many things in life you did or didn't do, or because you are the hapless victim of evil-doing assholes, or because you are trapped in a pathetic situation (family, marriage, school, work, health) with no future prospects. Maybe it's because you're fat, skinny, hairy, bald, ugly, stupid, ignorant, lazy, selfish, hateful, weak, incompetent, broken-down, boring, or just plain invisible. Maybe you believe life is pointless, and/or the injustice of human society is causing your misery.

Did I miss your purported reason? If so, summarize it below. The real reason I am depressed/anxious is...

_____

_____

_____

_____

_____

_____

_____

News Flash!

Any of these may indeed be the persistent triggers or themes of your miserable depression and anxiety, but *they are not the sustaining cause*. Let's discuss.

More than anything, we humans are *perceivers*. All our actions are driven by our perceptions. You may have been told that humans have five senses, but, for our purposes, we have at least eight:

1. Sight
2. Hearing
3. Touch

4. Smell
5. Taste
6. Proprioception (body position, motion, and equilibrium)
7. Awareness of thoughts
8. Awareness of feelings and emotions

While the first six senses stay active more or less constantly, most of their inputs are filtered by our attention. We attend selectively to the stimuli of the first six senses when we are awake.

Perhaps you disagree with my describing thoughts and feelings (seven and eight) as "senses" because they do not involve sensing the reality outside ourselves, as the first five do. Senses seven and eight are "internal perceptions" that we observe in a fashion similar to our external senses. Face it: We don't deliberately create thoughts and emotions any more than we generate smells or sights. Instead, we experience them, we observe them, we "have" them.

Number seven, *our awareness of having thoughts*, is by far the most consequential sense we experience from moment to moment. Your thoughts mediate between the incoming information from the first six senses and your resulting feelings and emotions (sense eight) and subsequent actions. You, *the consciousness who is miserable*, are "sensing" a continual stream of thoughts, whether you want to or not.

You might be able to shut off the first six senses by closing your eyes, plugging your ears and nose, and floating suspended in a saltwater bath, but there is no way in hell you can stop paying attention to the continuous flow of thoughts you perceive.

The Non-Stop Show in Your Head

As often as not, the first six senses do not actually determine your thoughts. Instead, memories or imaginary projections about the present, past, or future arise in your mind as "sensory thoughts" with no external source. These perceptions—i.e., daydreams—are completely internal, and they are continuous. You perceive a series of inbound thoughts, and you perceive subtle emotional reactions to them. You talk, act, or project; and then you perceive more thoughts and emotions in a never-ending "show" you watch in your mind.

Take one moment right now to observe yourself experiencing the show in your head. Stop thinking for a few seconds (if you can) and wait for the mind-show to start. Some single thought will pop up, followed by an associated thought of some kind, and, *zing*, the show is off and running of its own accord. You don't have to "do" anything but perceive it.

For example, right now you might think something like this: "OK, this is stupid, but I'll try it. [Two seconds of inner silence.] What? Nothing! I don't get it; I don't like this. I'm gonna get some food. Yeah, but I'm too fat, I really shouldn't. Ah, who cares, maybe just a snack. Let me check my phone first for..."

You and everyone you know grinds through life with a non-stop thought-show running in their heads. Whether they are standing in the shower, sitting at their desks, eating a meal, making love, or sitting on the toilet, their shows never stop for more than a nanosecond or two. Every person you pass on the street is busy watching their own head show. In that way, we are all alike. Incredible!

Shit Show

In your case, the show in your head is a shit show, and that's the root reason you are miserable (assuming you are not in immediate danger from an abuser, a rapist, or the Reaper). Let me repeat: *your life circumstances do not cause your misery. The 24/7 shit show in your head does.*

As a simple illustration of this truth, consider two cashiers working the graveyard shift, night after night at a convenience store, for minimum wage on a bleak, lonely interstate highway. Both work long hours for lousy pay. As the nights drag on, customers notice that one cashier is cheerful and upbeat, while the other is taciturn and surly—in other words, miserable. They both have shows going on in their heads, but only one has a shit show. Guess which one?

Now, before you whip up your resistance to this concept, remember that your resistance does not serve you. Hold your "yeah, but..." protests and hear me out. I will explain the thought/emotion loop that is torturing you, and then I'll give you the first four hacks that will provide palpable relief from your personal shit show.

The core engine of your personal shit show is your *thought-emotion loop*. Your incessant stream of unpleasant thoughts triggers a continual series of subtle emotional reactions in you. In other words, you don't just have one massive feeling of misery; you actually experience an endless stream of smaller, painful emotional "hits."

A normal head show becomes a *shit show* when, over an extended period of time, your thoughts generate a stream of emotional reactions that *feel shitty*. Each subtle, instantaneous emotion we experience falls somewhere within a range from joy to misery. You are miserable precisely because too many of your emotional reactions/perceptions fall closer to the misery end of the emotional scale. Let's call these the *shitty emotions*. Your myriad, subtle, shitty emotions are the enduring and sustaining source of your suffering.

You know what I'm talking about. You wake up when the alarm goes off, and your shit show cranks right up. "Ah, man, it's morning already? [ouch] Another night of lousy sleep! [ouch] I don't wanna get up yet. [ouch] Shit, I gotta get ready for work. [ugh] I hate my job! [ouch] Maybe if I had finished school I could've gotten something better… [ouch] Now, I'm stuck forever in this shit job. [aargh]. Ooh, I wanna get high…"

It took us a few pages to get here, so let me repeat: **You are miserable because you endure an endless stream of subtle, shitty feelings/emotions in response to certain thoughts that arise uninvited into your mind.**

What types of thoughts give rise to your shitty emotions? Well, obviously, *shitty thoughts*—the same few shitty thoughts over and over in an endless loop, or a wide variety of consistently shitty thoughts. You, like the rest of this book's readers and millions of others, have a shit show going on in your head around the clock. Try to shut off your shit show completely for even thirty seconds and you will fail!

This is the weird nature of human consciousness. The mind wanders fifty percent of the time. Yours, sadly, has wandered intractably into Shitsville. The *contents* of your thoughts, of course, include all the items listed above in your life circumstances: shitty job, shitty family, shitty friends, shitty past, shitty prospects, shitty body, shitty self. Let me assure you, though, if any of these circumstances change suddenly for the better, you will think shitty thoughts about something new within a very short time!

You might try to "change the channel" and declare your intention to generate some positive thoughts or affirmations, but, for whatever reason, the crappy thoughts reassert themselves almost immediately. Your life force suffers from death by a million shitty thoughts. Do you deny this?

If so, take just a few minutes and make a mark in the box below for every thought you have that *feels bad when it lands* in your awareness. It probably will start with, "This is a stupid idea."

Feel free to make a different mark for thoughts that feel uplifting when they land. The longer you do this, the more likely you are to agree with me that your life force is dying a tiny bit with each shitty thought.

Shitty thoughts   Happy thoughts

Your life force is so diminished at this point that all you can generate is shitty thoughts, right? (That realization is just another shitty thought, of course, that makes you feel even more miserable. Put a mark in the box!)

So, what are you going to do about this? You can start by forgetting about changing all of your life circumstances in one fell swoop. There will be time for life changes in the last three hacks. Instead, let's start implementing the first hack of *The Seven*.

Hack One: Micro-Slash

Hack One is the *Micro-Slash Hack*. It is hardly fun, but it is easy. It does not cure any of your problems; but it is indispensable to the next two hacks, which are massively powerful. You'll use the Micro-Slash Hack habitually for a long time to come, and you'll become an expert at this hack.

The micro-slash hack requires your immediate recognition of any thought that stimulates a shitty feeling.

In essence, each shitty feeling you experience in response to a shitty thought is one little "micro-slash" to your emotional well-being. Individually, one micro-slash is no big deal; perhaps you are not even aware of most of them. As you deploy this hack, though, you may be shocked to realize just how many slashes you are taking. These thousand micro-slashes you experience all day, every day, add up to the decimation and death of your life force.

Ironically, the Micro-Slash Hack does not require you to identify or analyze the contents of the shitty thoughts. In fact, it forbids you to! This means ignoring completely whether or not the shit show content has any value. Invest zero energy in separating fact from fiction, and do not engage with a single thing the voice is saying. We do not care if the thought is "true." We do not care if the thought has any merit at all! If it feels bad when it lands, it is part of your shit show, and therefore is part of the problem being hacked. Are you with me on this?

The Micro-Slash Hack requires you to notice *instantly* when you experience a shitty feeling following any thought. That's it. This is straightforward; in a very short time, you will be saying to yourself, "Ouch," "There's one," "Shit," "That hurt," etc.

Starting immediately, you will wage a persistent vigil for shitty thoughts and their shitty feelings. Take twenty or thirty seconds right now and see how many you get. Here's a short example of a teenage shit show:

"What kind of stupid idea is this? [ouch] I am wasting my time; this idiot can't help me [shit]. I have to do homework [fuck]; I hate school [ouch]. I can't drop out [that hurt] because my parents will make me move out. They suck! [ugh]"

See, I told you this was easy!

If you are more depressed than anxious, the contents of your shitty thoughts probably relate more towards your past and present, while thoughts that trigger anxiety often relate more to the present and future.

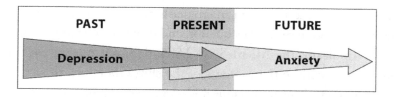

Close this book until tomorrow and practice your Micro-Slash Hack. You can count your shitty thought-emotion loops if you like. That should be entertaining until you reach fifty in the first half-hour or less. When that gets tiresome, you can stop counting, but *you must continue to acknowledge every micro-slash until it becomes unconsciously automatic.*

As I said, *Hack One* is no fun. Yes, it sucks to throw the bright light of awareness on the relentless stream of micro-slashes your personal shit show is raining down on you. Small wonder you are depressed and/or anxious!

I require your realization and agreement on how numerous and incessant these slashes are because the next two hacks fly in the face of traditional approaches to dealing with negative, unwanted thoughts. If you accept my claim that your personal shit show generates an unrelenting shit storm of micro-slashes to your life force, you'll be more open to implementing the next two hacks.

Don't be surprised or disappointed if implementing this hack generates even more shitty-thought-emotion loops. I'm willing to bet that you had at least a couple of shitty loops while you were reading these paragraphs. Persist anyway.

Please don't *do* anything about your micro-slashes, just yet. Remember, *no processing!* For example, do not say, "Damn, all my shitty feelings are about X, so I'm going to quit my job, get a divorce, buy a gun, spend my life's savings on lottery tickets..." For now, merely observe and acknowledge every micro-slash.

You will know you are really on the right track when you notice a shitty feeling arising a nanosecond *before* the actual shitty thought is fully formed in your mind! Yes, I am saying your body can and does react to incoming shitty thoughts before your conscious mind processes the verbal content into your awareness. If you register this experience, you are doing very well, and your future prospects just brightened. This might not happen immediately, but it will, soon enough.

A Little Good News

There's one good thing about counting your micro-slashes. You soon understand viscerally that *you are not your thoughts.* You're the miserable entity observing and acknowledging your shitty thoughts, but they are not you. You, the observer, stand apart from your thoughts and watch them fly by. As we work our way through *The Seven Life Hacks,* this observer will gain freedom, power, and life force.

In the meantime, shut the book and start counting your micro-slashes. I know you'll be absolutely transfixed by the insidious barrage of micro-slashes you endure. You don't have to overcome or stop this barrage—that will come in subsequent hacks—but you must become an ace at *Hack One,* acknowledging each micro-slash the instant you get cut.

The Surprising Source of Shitty Thoughts

Before unveiling the second hack—among the most potent of *The Seven*—I must provide some context. First, we'll ruminate about the source of your shitty thoughts. Then we'll briefly consider some traditional approaches to fixing the problem, and I'll explain why they don't serve you in your present state of misery. By that point, I expect you'll be reasonably receptive to the unusual nature of *Hack Two*.

Believe me, I am not trying to impress you or establish my creds here. I realize you are in a hurry to get to this game-changing hack and couldn't care less about my erudition. This mercifully brief section will establish that *Hack Two* is perhaps the only feasible method to curtail your mental misery, short of killing yourself (which might not work, anyway). Let's dive in.

The Source

Shitty or not, where do our thoughts come from? We perceive thoughts in much the same way we perceive sights, sounds, and odors in the external world, but many thoughts seem to be generated internally, irrespective of external conditions. Humans have exhibited abstract and symbolic thought for at least forty thousand—and maybe a couple of million—years, and it is reasonable to assume that early humans wondered where those thoughts came from. Therefore, humans have had millennia to investigate the compelling question, "Where do our thoughts come from?"

The answer? We have no frigging idea! If you expect to gain valuable insight by combing the abundant literature on this topic, don't waste your time: Nobody knows. Instead, just give me three or four pages here to summarize a handful of prevailing, if unproven, theories about what's going on inside our busy heads. Then I'll introduce my astounding, alternative explanation that we'll use to change your life for the better.

The modern, scientific perspective asserts that our physical brains create our mental thoughts. The field of cognitive neuroscience describes thoughts as a continual series of electro-chemical reactions occurring in the brain's one hundred billion neurons. In your brain's multi-layered architecture, conscious thoughts emerge into your awareness as distillations of the deeper, unconscious processing of electrical activity generated in trillions of neuronal connections throughout numerous modules of your brain. The complexity is mind-boggling.

Presently, though, little is known about how your brain "generates" your mind and its shit show of miserable thoughts and unhappy emotions. It's widely accepted that damage to certain modules or processes of the brain can dramatically alter and impair thinking, but specifically how thoughts are generated and experienced as consciousness remains a faith-based mystery.

This physical-system approach to shitty thoughts and feelings (that is, they're caused by unbalanced brain chemistry) allows psychiatrists to prescribe drugs to disrupt or inhibit these physiological thought processes, while greatly enriching the pharmaceutical industry. Perhaps you have tried these medications? Research suggests they are slightly more effective at reducing depression in the average patient than placebos with similar side effects.[1] They arguably are better than doing nothing, especially if you overlook their potentially unpleasant side effects.

However, hundreds of billions of dollars of medications have not solved the daunting problem of depression and anxiety in our society. Countless medicated people still suffer through their shit shows, all day, every day. And, for now at least, neuroscientists are still scratching their heads about exactly where in the brain thoughts originate and how we can eliminate the shitty ones.

It's also possible our thoughts are not generated internally by the machinations of our physical brains. For much of human history, people have believed in *external* sources for thoughts. Picture your brain as a radio that receives incoming signals and translates them, via electrical activity, into thoughts in your head.

OK, but *where* externally do thoughts come from? Again, we have no idea. Perhaps Satan's and God's angelic messengers are fighting for your immortal soul by whispering thoughts continually into your head, encouraging you to follow the right or wrong path to your eternal reward or damnation. Certainly,

---

[1] Ilardi, Stephen S. *The Depression Cure: The 6-step Program to Beat Depression without Drugs.* Cambridge, MA: Da Capo Lifelong, 2010. P. 46

millions, if not billions of folks throughout history have subscribed to explanations of this ilk, and many still do.

Another metaphysical explanation is that packets of thoughts just sit *out there* somewhere in non-physical clusters, and your personal energetic vibration attracts thoughts of similar frequencies. Higher frequency vibrations attract happier thoughts, which in turn stimulate higher internal vibrations, creating a positive feedback loop. Similarly, lower vibrations attract shitty thoughts, which make you feel shittier, attracting even worse thoughts. In this paradigm, falling into a funk is as treacherous as quicksand.

An especially popular metaphysical concept involves pairing the physical *you* with a non-physical part of yourself, such as your soul. Your "higher self" communicates with you via your thoughts and feelings. In this construct, folks having a lot of shitty thoughts are not living harmoniously with the desires of their higher selves. Shitty feelings are simply feedback that you are out of compliance with your soul's higher purpose.

Another long-standing approach says your physical body and brain comprise the locus for multiple entities or personalities who are struggling to co-exist. In this case, the thoughts in your head come from multiple voices, each with its own agenda.

Among the countless variations of this theme, Sigmund Freud dominated psychoanalytic theory with his description of the interminable battle between the conflicting, unconscious demands of the wild-child *id* and the parental *superego*, with the hapless *ego* suffering as forbearing mediator. Freud's protégé Carl Jung added a second level to our internal unconscious dimension: the *collective unconscious*, which further influences our thoughts through instinct and ancient archetypes.

A more recent variation on the multiplicity of sub-personalities jostling for control of the mind is the Internal Family Systems Model (IFS) developed by Richard Schwartz, Ph.D. Schwartz's model claims each individual's mind has an indeterminate number of parts that fall into the categories of *exiles, managers,* and *firefighters.* The intention of each part is something positive for the individual, but sometimes they carry burdens that force them to go to destructive extremes. It is the role of the *Self* to take the leadership position and create balance and harmony among the parts, similar to Freud's concept of the ego's role.[2]

---

[2] Schwartz, Richard C. *You Are the One You've Been Waiting For: Bringing Courageous Love to Intimate Relationships.* Oak Park, IL: Trailheads, 2008. IFS Family Systems Model (IFS)

The pinnacle of this intriguing concept of conflicting forces or personas vying for control in our heads comes from the creator of Alchemical Hypnotherapy, David Quigley, who developed a fascinating Conference Room Therapy for the twenty-four distinct sub-personalities fighting to grab the microphone in your head and "control your thoughts and destiny."[3]

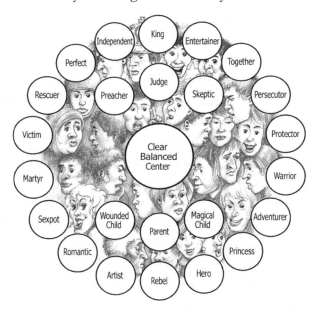

My point here is that you can spend your life investigating the many theories about where our thoughts come from—as I have—and you will probably conclude—as I have—that we will never know for certain. No matter their source, they just keep pouring in.

---

[3] Unterman, Debbie. *Talking to My Selves: Learning to Love the Voices in Your Head.* Charleston, SC: Booksurge.com, 2009.

Each of these hypotheses for the source of human thought has naturally suggested approaches for living happily. I will mention a couple shortly, but first let's consider one final, lesser-known, yet highly compelling metaphor for the true source of your shitty thoughts. I don't claim this source is more credible or true than any of those already mentioned, but *it can prove indispensable for ending your misery*, as it did mine. What I'm about to say might sound insane, but bear with me; there's a method to my madness.

Loosh, the Parasite, and the Foreign Installation

My first inkling of this insight came from Robert Monroe, author of three books and founder of the Monroe Institute in West Virginia. His second book, *Far Journeys*, chronicles his out-of-body interactions with highly intelligent, non-physical entities. In Chapter 12, Monroe introduces the term *loosh* to describe human emotional energy, and he surprisingly claims human loosh is "harvested" by non-physical entities as a highly useful source of creative energy.[4] In fact, we humans are basically farmed like cows, pigs, and chickens to produce loosh!

I was shocked at the prospect of not being at the top of the food chain. Despite my queasy discomfort, upon reflection, loosh explains many aspects of the human condition. Interpersonal dynamics, with associated love, compassion, fear, hatred, jealousy, and envy, create a bottomless cauldron of loosh. The dramatic differences in emotional and physical needs between men and women—such that men are from Mars and women are from Venus—is a perfect setup for rampant loosh production. Humans

---

4   Monroe, Robert A. *Far journeys*. New York: Harmony Books, 2016. Pp. 162-170.

emoting vigorously while lounging in front of a TV show or cheering in a sports arena are efficient generators of loosh in a safe environment. Wow, what a unique and mind-blowing concept! *Again, it doesn't matter for our purposes if this radical idea is true or completely nuts.* Either way, we can use it to your advantage, as I'll describe shortly.

The unnerving concept of *human emotions serving as energetic nutrition for non-physical entities* reappeared as I studied the radically different world view of the ancient Toltecs, as presented separately by both Carlos Casteneda and Miguel Ruiz. These two authors each describe a fascinating variation of inorganic beings who feed off the life force of humans.

In his mega-bestseller, *The Four Agreements: A Practical Guide to Personal Freedom* (which I bought on impulse in a Starbucks), Ruiz introduces the *parasite* as a living being made of psychic or emotional energy that invades the human mind and controls the brain, feeding on negative emotions that arise from fear. Comprised of a judge, a victim, and an associated belief system, "the parasite dreams through your mind and lives its life through your body. It survives on the emotions that come from fear, and thrives on drama and suffering."[5] Ruiz's four agreements help the reader become a warrior who rebels against the invasion of this energetic parasite.

Carlos Casteneda was an American anthropologist and best-selling author who, from 1960 to 1971, was an apprentice in Mexico to a Toltec sorcerer he called Don Juan. In *The Active Side of Infinity*, his eleventh book chronicling his initiations, Castaneda

---

[5] Ruiz, Miguel. *The Four Agreements: A Practical Guide to Personal Freedom*. San Rafael, CA: Amber-Allen, 1997. Pp. 101-105

recounts a stunning revelation Don Juan made about the non-physical entities he called the *foreign installation.*

> "We have a companion for life. We have a predator that came from the depths of the cosmos and took over the rule of our lives. Human beings are its prisoners. The predator is our lord and master. It has rendered us docile, helpless. If we want to protest, it suppresses our protest. If we want to act independently, it demands that we don't do so…. *They took over because we are food for them, and they squeeze us mercilessly because we are their sustenance. Just as we rear chickens in chicken coops, the predators rear us in human coops. Therefore, their food is always available to them.*"[6]

Echoing the ideas of Robert Monroe and Miguel Ruiz, Don Juan explains that the foreign installation feeds on our emotional energy, leaving us only the barest essence of life force needed to survive.

> "By playing on our self-reflection, which is the only point of awareness left to us, the predators create flares of awareness that they proceed to consume in a ruthless, predatory fashion. They give us inane problems that force those flares of awareness to rise, and in this manner they keep us alive in order for them to be fed with the energetic flare of our pseudoconcerns."[7]

6   Castaneda, Carlos. *The Active Side of Infinity.* London: Harper Perennial, 2000. Pp. 218-219
7   Ibid. p. 221

Your immediate reaction, like mine, might be, "Holy hell, this is mega-depressing!" Can this outlandish assertion actually be true? We might never know. And, as I said earlier, *it doesn't matter*, so please don't worry about that. True or not, the ideas of loosh, the parasite, and the foreign installation provide your first ticket to freedom from your misery and the reinvigoration of your life force.

Because you resist new ideas and I really want you to entertain this one, let me say this: We live in a ridiculous world where creatures—including you—eat each other as a source of energy. You have trillions of microscopic organisms feeding off various parts of your body right now. You accept this because science told you so, and you soldier on, hoping none of these *unseen creatures* overwhelm your immune system and kill you.

If you are like most other folks, you also believe that humankind was created by a *non-physical entity* beyond our comprehension for god-knows-what reason. You might even accept the explanation that "the reason" is a life-long behavioral test to decide whether your (*also non-physical*) soul spends eternity in bliss or hell-fire.

So, tell me, is it really that big a stretch to say your shitty thoughts are coming from an unseen entity that is feeding off your unhappy emotions? Is it, really?

If it still is—or if you simply cannot tolerate the thought—then just consider the whole concept a useful metaphor.

You are bombed relentlessly by shitty thoughts from an unknown source. For now, at least, let's assume this loosh/parasite/foreign installation idea is as good an explanation as any about the source of your miserable thoughts. Let's say your brain chemistry, your genetic disposition, your unfortunate childhood experiences, the annoying people in your life, or your own lousy luck or shortcomings are not responsible for your life-sapping depression and/or anxiety. Your "foreign installation" is literally eating you alive!

Let's personify your foreign installation and call it **The Beast**. Yes, our working assumption for *Hack Two* is that The Beast is the source of your shitty thoughts. Warm up to it. It puts the responsibility for your shit show onto a nefarious third party, which instantly gives you a tiny measure of relief. YOU are not screwed up... *YOU are under attack!* Instead of a mysterious source or a dark, uncaring universe, you possess your very own Beast!

In fact, it's possible the folks with the brightest life force attract the most vicious Beasts, right? Perhaps you are being tortured by far more shitty thoughts than the average person because your once-awesome life force lured a more rapacious Beast!

As you contemplate this mind-bending idea, perhaps you want to customize your image of your personal life-force-parasite and give yours a name of your choosing. An old friend of mine, Peter Mucha, invented several clever ones: Stormentor, Craptor, PsyKick, Demoralizer, and Shitzonya. Feel free to draw a picture of your very own Beast and write its name in large letters in the box below. Have a little fun with it, if you can.

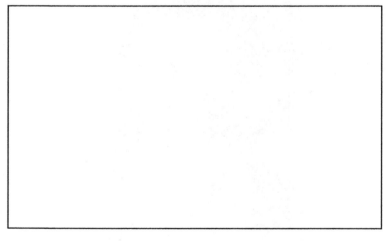

Ironically, The Beast—or whatever you're now calling your foreign installation— *has no real power or formal dominion over you.* It cannot control your actions or emotions. All your Beast can do is pummel you perpetually with shitty thoughts.

So why do these shitty thoughts from The Beast feel bad when they land? These thoughts hurt because you give *authority* to the source, even though you have no idea what it is. Let's face the facts: you pay homage and give credence to an asshole embedded in your mind, who makes you miserable by constantly criticizing you, your life, and everything going on around you. You give The Beast power to make you miserable because you *care* about what it says.

I am not saying your shitty life circumstances (job/school, money, health, relationships, and appearance issues) or existential concerns are irrelevant to your depression/anxiety. No, I am saying they provide the ammunition The Beast fires down on you. The smaller your actual problems, the harder The Beast will work to drum up shit to torture you with. That's why successful, good-looking, healthy, popular, rich people can still be miserably depressed.

So, humor me for now, and accept the unconventional assertion that your shitty thoughts are imposed on you by a nefarious, non-physical force beyond your comprehension. What approaches are best for banishing these shitty thoughts?

The Search for Relief

For at least the last 150 years, and maybe as far back as the ninth century, humans have relied on some form of talk therapy to relieve depression and anxiety. Typically, the therapeutic alliance between a patient and therapist involves lots of talking by the patient, while the therapist guides the patient to insights leading to potential improvement of thoughts and relief of shitty emotions. I won't go into the many permutations since Freud popularized talk therapy in the late 1800s, because these are easily found on the web.

In recent decades, cognitive behavioral therapy (CBT) has emerged as an effective form of talk therapy, and a patient can even learn to implement CBT techniques without the presence of a therapist. As a vast oversimplification, CBT involves examining automatic negative thoughts, identifying distortions or untruths in the thinking, and substituting a rational response.

For example, if your daughter gets sick and you feel shitty because your thoughts insist you're a failure as a parent, you use a CBT technique to identify the thought as one of ten or more types of twisted thinking, such as jumping to conclusions, overgeneralization, or labeling. You then substitute the thought with a more rational response, such as, "Hey, all kids get sick from time to time, and I actually am a very dedicated, caring parent. Ah, that feels better."

CBT is a wonderful advance in psychotherapy. It is very useful for some, but not for you, not now. Why not?

Two reasons. First, CBT involves too much exhausting mental work. You lack sufficient life force to take on each of the thousand or more micro-slashes you get hit with each day—write it down, identify the type of twisted thinking, and substitute a more rational thought. You'll be mentally wiped out a half hour after breakfast, and you'll never have time to do anything else.

Second, lots of the shitty thoughts you have are true! There is no twisted thinking involved. If you look in the mirror at your body that is fifty pounds overweight, your Beast will say, "You are a fat ass!" There is no rational response to substitute. Trying and failing to find one gives your Beast more material to slash you with. So forget CBT for now.

A simpler approach to responding proactively to shitty thoughts is The Law of Attraction, popularized by Esther Hicks (channeling a non-physical entity called Abraham) and later by the movie and book, *The Secret*. In a nutshell, each thought has an emotional vibration that corresponds to a spot on a scale of twenty-two emotions. At the bottom are the emotions of fear/grief/depression/despair/powerlessness, and at the top are joy/appreciation/empowerment/freedom/love. A thought that stimulates a feeling from the bottom of the emotional scale is feedback that you are not in harmony with your "higher self."[8]

The Law of Attraction solution to shitty thoughts is a lot easier than CBT because you only have to *find a thought that feels just a little bit better*. The better feeling thought doesn't even need to be related to the shitty thought. Your response to "I am a fat ass" or "I am a lousy parent" could be, "Jeez, I am excited about going bowling tonight!" As long as it feels better, you are on the road to raising your vibrational frequency, and you will attract more positive thoughts.

I became enamored of this approach and employed it assiduously for several years. If an acquaintance asked what I was up to lately, I'd say, "I am finding a thought that feels better!" I liked that each micro-slash from The Beast did not require engagement or rationalization. I could simply change the channel from whatever shit The Beast was dumping on me to a happier line of thought. Without conflict, I could just segue from feeling anxious about

---

[8] Hicks, Esther, and Jerry Hicks. *Ask and It is Given: Learning to Manifest Your Desires*. New Delhi, India: Hay House Publications (India) Pvt. Ltd., 2017.

my dead-end job to simply being glad the rain had stopped or the commute traffic was moving. It also gave rise to *Hack One*, because it helped me identify the instantaneous connection between each thought and its corresponding feeling.

However, as with CBT, "happy thoughts" and the myriad related approaches to reframing thinking can only take you so far. It is exhausting to be on a continual search for a better feeling thought, and sometimes those are hard to come by. Shitty thoughts resurface persistently. Sifting frantically through a bushel of crappy thoughts in hope of finding just one good one traps the vibrational frequency at anxious. At some point in the future, CBT and finding happier thoughts might serve you well, but more draconian measures are called for right now in the battle of The Beast. Press on to *Hack Two!*

Hack Two: Bitch-Slap

Hack Two should change your life for the better. You will be a different person. Your life force will revive, and your misery will begin slinking permanently into your past.

With that stirring intro out of the way, let me insist that you can proceed to *Hack Two* only if you are impressively adept at *Hack One*. If instead, you are plowing into this chapter without proving you can recognize every micro-slash the instant it lands, you are a poser who is unlikely to benefit noticeably from this powerful hack. Therefore, it's time for another checkbox challenge.

Pick one now:

☐   I kept reading without mastering *Hack One*. The whole idea of it sucked, and I did not feel like noticing every god-damned shitty feeling I had. (Either go back and master *Hack One* or return the book for a refund.)

☐   Oh yeah, I now am painfully aware of each shitty thought-feeling as it lands, and actually, I am getting pretty pissed off that you made me focus on how screwed up my mind is. (OK, continue, you are doing great.)

☐ *Hack One* blew me away. What do I do now? (Proceed, my friend.)

Bitch-Slapping The Beast

Merriam Webster's online dictionary defines the slang term "bitch-slap" as a transitive verb meaning *"to slap (someone) angrily usually as an expression of dominance, contempt, or disrespect,"* and that's exactly what I am talking about in this hack.

Does the term "bitch-slap" annoy you? I hope so, because I want you annoyed now. Being annoyed will prove far more useful than being glum or morose. You *should* be pissed off, having just realized an invisible, energetic beast is force-feeding you shitty thoughts and devouring your life force. (This is almost worse than shoving corn down tubes in the throats of geese to fatten their livers for *foie gras...* just sayin'.)

Despite requiring an excruciating degree of diligence, *Hack Two* is simple, easy, and—yes—fun! You must have realized by now that trying to reason with The Beast is a fool's gambit. The only sensible solution to your mental suffering is to bitch-slap The Beast every time it force-feeds you a shitty thought.

Let me be crystal clear: from now on, *any* and *every* thought that feels shitty when it lands is to be immediately resisted, rejected, and repudiated! ***You repulse each micro-slash the instant it strikes.*** Every time The Beast tries to land a micro-slash, you bitch-slap The Beast, immediately.

Do not take even one second to analyze whether a shitty-feeling thought is true or has value to you. If you try, The Beast will outmaneuver you every time. Instead, your *Hack Two* intent is to instinctively and reflexively reject the inbound shit before it sticks.

Don't entertain it, don't explore it, don't process it, don't accept it with loving kindness, don't play patty-cake, patty cake with it. If a thought feels shitty, immediately *bitch-slap The Beast!*

How do you bitch-slap a non-physical entity? It depends on your manner of thinking. Visual thinkers can imagine bitch-slapping or nose-punching a hulking beast. Perhaps you prefer to slap The Beast with a fly-swatter or smack it with a heavy pillow, a black-jack, or a baseball bat. Use your imagination!

Because I am a verbal thinker, I bitch-slap The Beast verbally. Here are a few examples. Compare their simplicity to the complexity and rigor of CBT techniques and "finding happier thoughts".

Thought	Feeling	Bitch-Slap Response
• "I don't want to go to work today."	Shitty	"Shut up!"
• "I can't stand to look at myself in the mirror."	Shitty	"Shut the hell up!"
• "It's supposed to snow again today."	Shitty	"Piss off!"
• "How am I gonna pay this bill?"	Shitty	"Leave me alone!"
• "I miss my ex-boyfriend/ girlfriend."	Shitty	"Fuck off!"
• "You'll never amount to anything."	Shitty	"Who asked you!"
• "You're (I'm) a worthless loser."	Shitty	"You suck!"
• "I'm the only honest person left in the world."	Shitty	"Stop already!"
• "That floor needs refinishing."	Shitty	"Blow it out your ass!"

The concept I want to drive home is this: *the specific contents of your thoughts are completely, entirely, and utterly irrelevant to* **Hack Two.** Can I say it any more clearly?

Don't fear that you might be suppressing or repressing your feelings to your ultimate detriment. *Hack One* helped you recognize at once how you feel: shitty! That is all the "processing" you need. Now, you are going to fight back.

Because you have already mastered *Hack One*, you easily identify incoming thoughts destined to cause shitty feelings. You are more than ready to deploy *Hack Two*, by immediately responding, "Shut the heck/hell/fuck up!" Instead of meekly taking the thousands of micro-slashes, or trying to dissect and reframe each one, you now will generate enough annoyance, anger, and hostility to slap down the thought and its beastly source.

This is true crisis intervention. It must happen the instant any thought lands and generates the slightest negative feeling, before you start to process the content mentally and allow it turn into a bona fide emotion. As you get more skilled, you will sometimes notice the shitty feeling even before the thought has fully formed. When you do, pounce immediately and verbally punch The Beast in the nose: "Shut the hell up!"

Develop a certain poise, like a vigilant jail guard ready to whack a prisoner who gets out of line. Relatively soon, your bitch-slap mental program will run in the background, ever alert. This process will give you a long-lost feeling of relief, of freedom, of power.

I admit this sounds ridiculously simple, simplistic, or silly, which is why I went through the whole rigmarole about the source of our thoughts and traditional approaches for improving them. Just to rehash: We have no idea where thoughts come from; we live in a world where creatures eat each other to survive; we believe in non-physical entities; and your life force is being decimated by a relentless stream of thoughts that make you feel shitty. So why not give *Hack Two* a try, and start a little bitch-slapping? What have you got to lose? You might like it. I know I do.

Your Resistance

I hope you are embracing *Hack Two*, but I know you're probably resisting it. I say this because you are basically a very nice person; too nice, in fact, and you know that. Maybe you wear your niceness like a badge of suffering. "I'm just too nice [shitty feeling]... people take advantage of me [shitty feeling]." Let's face it, most depressed and anxious people *are* too nice, and most assholes are *not* depressed and anxious. You probably resist repeatedly shouting, "Shut the hell up!" even to your own thoughts, right?"

Perhaps you're clinging to the quaint idea that your thoughts are important messages from God, your guardian angel, your spirit guide, your soul, your higher self, or some other source that's trying to help you. Well, how's that been working out for you?

Now's the time for you to make the change I asked of you at the beginning of this book. It is time for the force of life to flow in the opposite direction—*to* you, not *from* you. You are going to be nasty to The Beast from now on, until The Beast is just as whipped as you are now. Don't try merely to ignore The Beast; that is fruitless. You must be more aggressive and vigilant than if you were protecting a loved one from evil incarnate. Your life force is that important.

In the beginning, you will say a lot of spiteful things to The Beast, and this nastiness might annoy you. You might move through your day mildly annoyed to seriously pissed off, depending upon you how many micro-slashes you are taking and how much bitch-slapping you are doing. This is good because anger contains more life force than depression and anxiety. Embrace your anger as a crucial step on your journey to Neutral.

Perhaps you aren't ready to bitch-slap The Beast because you have a few "what-ifs." What if the bad feeling is a warning that I shouldn't go out with that guy because he's a serial killer? What if this awful feeling is because I know eating that triple banana split will aggravate my diabetes? What if that mole on my nose really is cancerous? What if I feel shitty because stealing cash from my mom's purse is a sin? What if I feel bad because I am afraid I'll get arrested for beating the crap out of my spouse/sibling/classmate/boss/neighbor's dog?

Although my knee-jerk reaction is to reply with the same panache I give The Beast—"Shut up, asshole!"—I admit that sometimes your shitty thoughts and feelings have real value. You can take a moment to consider this, right *after* you bitch-slap The Beast!

Our BHAG (big, hairy-assed goal) is not to be reasonable and to play fair with The Beast; it is to resurrect your vital life force. Forget all the what-ifs and focus on owning the habit of reflexively repelling every shitty thought before its shitty feeling takes another whack at your feeble life force.

What to Expect

So, what can you expect to happen as you become adroit at bitch-slapping The Beast? In the very beginning, expect The Beast to ramp up its rate of slashing as it struggles to maintain control over you. You might find yourself saying some variation of "shut up!" dozens of times in rapid succession. (*Hack Three* will help with this.) Saying "shut up" is a lot less tiring than using

CBT techniques or finding happier thoughts, though. You might start to feel frustrated and wonder if you can persist with constant bitch-slapping. You can and you must.

Suddenly, though, something wonderful will happen. After a bitch-slap, you will perceive something new: a moment or two of absolute silence. It will seem as though someone has lifted the needle off the vinyl record of shitty thoughts playing in your head. Your body and mind (prepped for another shitty feeling) will experience an instant of confusion and maybe a shudder of exhilaration. Wait, what, the shit show stopped!? Silence? Whew! *Wow!*

When your shit storm stops, what should you do? For now, just observe and enjoy the brief but profound silence. Feel the empty space. Acknowledge the *you* experiencing the quiet stillness. Maybe a tiny, almost imperceptible whiff of life force will blossom, bringing a subtle feeling of relief. Yes, there is hope. The Beast can be tamed. Ah, that silence feels good!

See how long the stillness stretches before the show starts again. (*Hack Four* adds some other ideas.) Before long, the micro-slashes and bitch-slapping will resume.

Will the micro-slashes ever stop? Can The Beast be utterly vanquished? I have bad news and good news. In my experience, The Beast cannot be killed. It will be with you always, waiting for any opportunity to pounce and devour your precious life force. The good news—and the reason I am writing this book for you—is that you can beat The Beast into submission, dramatically reducing the number of shitty thoughts and feelings, freeing up mental and emotional space to enjoy positive experiences, and consistently banishing your depression and anxiety. *Hack Two* is the linchpin of *The Seven*. When you master *Hack Two*, your life will become forever better.

Before we move on, try a little exercise. Write down your three or four shittiest repetitive thoughts and what you are going to say to The Beast the next time they surface.

Thought	Feeling	Bitch-Slap Response

You don't have to put this book down after this chapter, because *Hack Three* goes hand-in-hand with *Hack Two*, and you will deploy them simultaneously to defeat The Beast. That said, taking a day or two to practice *Hack Two* before proceeding will help you appreciate the value of *Hack Three*.

Hack Three: Diversion

Assuming you are aligned with me thus far, you are sensing the myriad micro-slashes continually bleeding out your life force, and you are bitch-slapping The Beast aggressively and often. You feel more alert and alive than before you picked up this book. Perhaps you've won a moment or two of wonderful silence, as the stunned Beast shut the hell up. Have you? If so, you are on the program and succeeding nicely.

Hack Three makes your job a little easier. Although bitch-slapping requires far less energy than psychotherapy, CBT techniques, or finding happier thoughts, it still wears you out over the course of hours, days, and weeks. Each and every micro-slash requires a bitch-slap; therefore, we need to reduce your "micro-slashes per hour" metric.

The vast majority of The Beast's micro-slashes occur when your mind wanders from whatever you are doing in the present moment. One thought associated with the task at hand generates an associated thought, then another, and—*zoom*—you are off in a mental daydream from which The Beast extracts a bucket of shit to rain down on you.

For example, imagine you are rinsing dishes in the sink, minding your own business. You think, "Ah, there's still some food on that dish. If I don't get it all off, Erica will bitch about it out later [ouch]. She's *always* complaining about whatever I do [crap]. She gave me shit last night just because I left my dirty socks on the coffee table [slash]. Then she yelled at me for picking at my toes while I watched TV, the stupid bitch [growl]. Hey, it's my place, too. I wish I could throw her out, but I can't afford the rent [ouch] because of my crappy, dead-end job [crap]..." The shit show runs on endlessly whenever your mind wanders.

How often does your mind wander? Oh, about forty-seven to seventy-five percent of the time, depending on which researchers you believe. Conservatively, let's say half your waking hours, or about eight hours per day, are spent daydreaming. You are battling The Beast most of that time, are you not? We need a hack to reduce your mind-wandering, daydreaming moments.

You might expect me to recommend "mindfulness" now, but I will not. No doubt, keeping your attention on whatever activity your physical senses are attending to in the present moment, is a popular prescription for a happier mind. From Buddhist meditation techniques to Ram Dass's *Be Here Now* and Eckhart Tolle's *The Power of Now*, mindfulness is all the rage. I like it too, but it is not for you. Like CBT and happier thoughts, mindfulness requires too much energy and attention from someone severely lacking in life force. Don't bother with it, at least for "now."

Instead, deploy *Hack Three: Diversion* to reduce daydreaming by fifty percent or more. Get ready to enjoy a lot fewer micro-slashes and a lot less bitch-slapping. **Hack Three** *diverts your attention to activities that reduce your daydreaming.* That's it. These activities might include playing sports, playing music, reading, listening to audiobooks, watching TV, playing video games, surfing digital media on your phone, doing crafts, gardening, exercise, sex, and so on.

The critical differentiator is, your *mind must wander less into the territory of shitty thoughts* while you are doing the activity. If you can play basketball or the guitar for two hours with nary a peep from The Beast, you are diversion-hacking successfully. In contrast, if The Beast relentlessly calls you a worthless loser as you surf your phone or play video games, then you must find another activity that holds more of your attention. For example, I embraced hiking through a redwood forest in a nearby state park to reduce stress. Unfortunately, I often wasted most of the hike running some shit show through my head in an effort to "process my issues." Then I discovered a smartphone app that let me download free audiobooks from my local library. I first tried hiking while listening to personal development and spiritual growth audiobooks. They were only slightly helpful because the contents frequently triggered associated thoughts about myself that The Beast would use to slash me. My mind still wandered too much.

I segued into suspenseful spy novels and historical fiction with superior results. I daydreamed much less. I also discovered that it usually took me thirty to ninety seconds to realize my attention had wandered. I'd reset the audio and refocus on the story, and my shit show would shut down entirely for another few minutes. My hikes became relaxing and reinvigorating.

Your resistance (probably generated by your Beast, by the way) might be protesting, "Yes, but distracting your mind from your present moment is a cop-out. It won't solve your problems. You should be doing something productive to improve your lot in life or to contribute to the world... blah, blah, blah."

OK, that might be fine advice for folks who are not quasi-suicidal from their mental shit shows. However, diversion solves a serious problem for the unfortunate souls saddled with vicious Beasts. It adds a potent tool for rebooting and restoring vital life force, which is our goal *numero uno*! You'll gain the initiative and mental stamina to find new, grander challenges after your emotional set point rises up and stabilizes at Neutral and beyond.

Overdoing Diversion

A related but more serious objection relates to overdoing diversion: "I play video games for fifteen hours straight every day, with no hassles from The Beast. But when I stop playing, The Beast devours me alive because I have no job, no money, no education, and no friends. I live like a slob, I need a bath, and I am about to be evicted." I'll have more to say about these life issues in the second half of this book, but for now let's say that diversion can be overused, to the ultimate detriment of your life force. Diversion gives you relief from your constant bitch-slapping, but it is not a dispensation from the basic responsibilities of animating a physical body on planet Earth. Diversion helps you rise up, not run away.

Notice, too, that I didn't include drugs or alcohol as useful diversions. In moderation, they can prove hella-useful, but the risk of overuse taints them severely. If you play far too much golf, or piano, or canasta, your life circumstances might deteriorate and your life force might diminish further. But if you wildly overdo drugs or alcohol, you'll enter a tempestuous black hole from which you and your (remaining) loved ones may never emerge.

As a final caution, make sure your chosen diversion actually does reduce The Beast's micro slashes. For example, you might think thumbing through your Instagram feed for ten or twelve hours a day is a useful diversion, while in fact The Beast is using the unending images of (apparently) beautiful people sharing joyous moments to remind you that your life totally sucks in comparison. If so, put down the damn device and choose another diversion. After a few days, you might be shocked to learn you're better off without it.

Ideally, deploy diversions that have some redeeming value in themselves, while effectively holding The Beast at bay. For example, *aerobic exercise generates pleasurable endorphins and is widely believed to help banish depression.* Reading broadens the mind. Music soothes the soul. Gardening beautifies your surroundings. Doing art, crafts, and projects stimulates feelings of satisfaction. Volunteering your time in service to others bestows a feeling of connection and a sense community. Learning a completely new skill requires focused attention and can prove more uplifting than habitual activities, so add a couple of new items to your list of diversions.

Review the list below and select two or more diversion activities to test for effectiveness in reducing The Beast's micro-slashes and boosting your life force. Use the most potent diversions as often as possible, in concert with frequent Beast-bitch-slapping, and monitor your emotional set point as it rises slowly from the depths of your miserable shit show.

Diversions

- ☐ exercising
- ☐ playing sports
- ☐ playing music
- ☐ reading or listening to audio books
- ☐ volunteering in your community
- ☐ creating art or crafts
- ☐ gardening
- ☐ having sex
- ☐ doing puzzles (newspaper or apps)
- ☐ creative writing
- ☐ singing and dancing
- ☐ conversing with non-judgmental friends

- ☐ attending AA or Al-anon meetings
- ☐ attending adult or evening school courses
- ☐ _____
- ☐ _____
- ☐ _____

Prime Time Diversions

Hack Three also has a time/place aspect. As you implemented Hacks One and Two, you probably identified a few times in your daily routine when The Beast attacks most aggressively. This is "prime time" in your personal shit show. For example, maybe first thing upon waking, as you lie in bed, The Beast goes ape-shit crazy and pounds you mercilessly with shitty thoughts. Perhaps The Beast is most aggressive on your daily commute, or while you are eating, working, or getting ready for bed. Figure out when your hottest, prime-time shit show episodes occur every day.

How should you react to prime-time assaults? Well, you can ramp up your anger and aggressively yell "shut up, shut up, shut up, *shut up!*" Or you can divert your ass out of that environment immediately! Jump out of bed as soon as you wake up, without waiting for the shit show to start. If The Beast continues slashing as you start your morning routine, deploy one of your diversion tactics, such as listening to an audiobook or the BBC or watching YouTube, a soap opera, or the History Channel on your tablet or smartphone as you groom.

Diverting your attention from daydreaming and reducing your prime-time exposure to micro-slashes are two easy and effective ways to diminish the relentless force of your shit storm.

Do not rush to the next chapter just yet. Give bitch-slapping and diversion hacking a few days, at least. Be strategic. Focus on reducing the total number of micro-slashes that comprise your personal shit show. Can you lower them by half? Yes, you can!

Diversion-hacking also ameliorates your growing annoyance with the need for constant bitch-slapping. You might settle into a higher emotional set point than you've felt for a long time. Your relief from the shit storm will encourage you.

Your next hack is the last of our hacks for improving the dynamics of your inner world. *Hack Four* will nudge your emotional set point even higher. Then, in the second half of the book, we will explore three new hacks for owning your external world.

Put this book down for a few days, and return when you feel some improvement in your emotional set point as a result of your bitch-slapping and diversion hacking.

Hack Four: Feeling Good-ish

I have to ask: did you invest some time implementing the diversion hack in your daily routine, or did you simply steam ahead into this chapter?

You are ready for *Hack Four only* if you can honestly say you are experiencing moments of absolute silence in your shit storm, moments when the stunned Beast shuts up, however briefly, as a result of your diversion and bitch-slapping. If you can't yet feel that silence, go back, reread the last two chapters and practice your hacks.

Hack Four sends us on a search for wisps of good feelings to fill that brief silence. If you're tempted to blow through this hack or skip it entirely, please don't. *Hack Four: Feeling Good-ish* lifts you above the continuous, epic battle with The Beast and awakens your ability to direct your thoughts to a more pleasant place. I implore you to read *Hack Four* and actually use it, starting today!

As you practiced *Hack One: Micro-Slash*, you gained skill at recognizing thoughts that feel shitty as they land. Have you also observed an occasional thought that feels *good,* or at least *good-ish*? Maybe one in a thousand? Yes, every once in a while a good feeling bubbles up, however tiny. It happens most often when you are distracted by something you enjoy doing, or at least feel neutral about, such as cooking a meal, exercising, creating or repairing something, or walking the dog. Can you recall one itsy-bitsy good feeling?

If not, keep a lookout for a short, subtle, pleasant feeling that sneaks up on you.

If you can think of one, are you surprised to realize you typically squash it instantaneously? For example, you are biking, or running, or driving, letting your attention wander, and one of those endless thought/feeling loops suddenly feels... wait... what?... kinda *good*! Perhaps you are thinking about a guy you met recently, and the thought, "I think he likes me" generates a nice feeling.

Before it even settles in, though, you crush it, shut it down. "Nah, he probably just wants to get laid, like every other male on the planet!" Result? Good feeling immediately turns into shitty feeling.

Or maybe you notice a stock or mutual fund you bought recently had a nice uptick in value. Hey, that was easy money! Then you immediately think, "So what, that doesn't begin to make up for all the shitty investments I've made." Or, "Crap, that won't even cover the cost of the fender bender I had on my car last week."

Your first realization of this reflexive shutting down of good-ish feelings can be shocking, unsettling, even dumbfounding. What the hell?

Don't dwell on it, though; recognize the shut down as another technique The Beast uses to devour your life force. Then deploy the first technique of *Hack Four* and *simply acknowledge and appreciate the good feeling.* A simple "thank you" is perfect. You just increased your life force a tiny bit!

Do not fall into wondering why you had a good feeling. That question is The Beast trying to slash you and take it away. Accept it and wait for a tiny spark of gratitude that indicates an infinitesimal increase in life force.

There is little more to say about this first technique of *Hack Four: Feeling Good-ish.* You expand *Hack One* to include acknowledging the occasional good-feeling thought the instant it lands, and you take a few seconds to possess and appreciate each one. Maybe nod your head and make a half-hearted attempt at a smile. Sigh if you want. That's it. These few upbeat seconds provide a wonderful respite from continual micro-slash hacking and bitch-slapping!

(Of course, it helps to be alert for patterns. If several feel-good moments happen during a specific activity—listening to music, joking with friends, or exercising, for example—move that diversion higher on your list of favorites.)

Insert Appreciation

The second feel-good technique comes into play during those brief moments when the bitch-slapped Beast shuts up for a few seconds. Earlier, I suggested you merely enjoy the silence until The Beast starts harassing you again. Now I recommend you use the empty space to tweak your life force by *deliberately inserting a thought of your own making.*

What kind of thought? Initially, I want you to appreciate something. Anything, actually. The first thing that comes to mind will do nicely. As long as you feel at least a tiny whiff of appreciation, you cannot get this wrong.

You might find it easier to simply look for something in the present moment, as opposed to searching your memory for something to appreciate. For example, if you're staring into the mirror and you think, "I'm glad that butt-ugly zit on my nose is smaller this morning," I applaud your effort.

For those times when nothing in the present moment seems worth appreciating, grab the first positive thought that comes to mind. If you think, "I am glad the military-industrial complex hasn't started a thermonuclear war today," I say you are feel-good hacking like a pro.

Again, the content of the thought you generate is immaterial, just as the contents of the shit storm The Beast hurls at you are irrelevant to our purposes. All we care about is your using the momentary silence to uplift your life force a milliamp or two by generating a little appreciation.

Try it, right now. I bet your Beast will shut up for a few seconds just to see if you can pull this off. You *can* do this, no matter how dark your mood. If you can't generate enough enthusiasm to say, "I admit the sunshine does look nice on those flowers," you can fall back on, "Jeez, I'm glad there isn't a giant rat gnawing on my big toe right now." You feel me?

Exclamation-Point It!

For an extra jolt of energy, see if you can put an exclamation point on your upbeat thought. For example, "That's a nice sunset. I mean, *damn*, that's a *nice* sunset!" If you have succeeded at generating a decent thought of appreciation, you'll probably agree it only takes a small additional effort to slap that exclamation point on it. Try it. It's fun!

Sometimes your life force might be so depleted that you cannot drum up any genuine appreciation to insert into your wonderful moment of beastly silence. That is OK. Can you think of anything that adds infinitesimally to that tiny feeling of relief you just had? It might be a sarcastic thought, a sexual fantasy, or an upbeat memory. The objective is to *use your mental creativity* to generate a thought that you like; one that adds incrementally to your life force in this very moment.

Wait, am I asking you to "find a thought that feels better?" You thought I had dispensed with that, right? Yes, I did say attempting to counter every shitty thought with one that feels better is utterly exhausting, and much more depleting than continuous bitch-slapping. I say this from years of personal experience with both techniques, so you can trust me on this.

That said, finding just one good-feeling thought to fill the occasional moment of precious silence in your shit show is not hard at all, and it gives you a powerful tonic on your road to Neutral and beyond. In the beginning, especially, moments of beastly silence are relatively few, so you'll probably have sufficient energy to generate a little appreciation or another thought that feels good. I know you will.

Then What?

What should you do immediately *after* your brief sensation of appreciation? If you're lucky, you might be able to string together two or three thought-feelings of appreciation before your mind wanders into territory The Beast finds fertile for feasting on your life force once again. Recommence bitch-slapping, as necessary.

Those few feelings of appreciation have real power, though. They nudge your emotional set point up a tiny bit, like a half-full helium balloon drifting slowly and erratically toward the ceiling. They prove, right now, that you actually possess the power to improve your mood, however slightly.

The *Feeling Good-ish Hack* is the easiest of *The Seven*. Look for small breaks in your shit storm and fill each with a thought that stimulates a spark of appreciation. Over time, these thoughts might become deeply moving, such as profound love for another being or heartfelt respect for some aspect of yourself. For now, though, the thoughts can be goofy, sappy, ridiculous, nonsensical, or ironic—as long as you get that short, sweet balm of appreciation.

Blessings

For a little variety, try our second option for proactively filling that tiny, empty thought-space: bless somebody or something. It does not have to be a person in your life; you could bless Mother Teresa, or Gandhi, or Madame Curie. Bless a superhero, an animal, a tree, or even your bicycle. Just use that brief silence to send a little jolt of warm, caring energy off to someone or something, somewhere in the multi-dimensional universe.

Add Intent

As more mental and emotional space opens up to you, consider adding *intent* to your bag of tricks. In that silence between Beast attacks, declare something you want to be, have, or do *that feels good* when you think it. Your statement of intent can be specific, such as "I will receive a new job/car/lover/tattoo," or it can be general, such as "My life is improving continually." Any intent that feels good is acceptable; so immediately discard any statements that feel lousy.

If the concept of inserting intent into the empty space between shitty thoughts feels daunting or annoying, forget about it for now. Stick with finding something to appreciate or bless, and the intent will arise of its own accord in due time.

Fifteen-Second TBI Routine

Perhaps you find it relatively easy to fill The Beast's occasional, momentary silence with a bit of appreciation, blessings, or intent of your own invention. If so, congratulations are in order.

You now qualify for the trifecta technique of *Hack Four: Feeling Good-ish*.

You're likely to forget this little trick by the time you finish the chapter, but I want you to try it at least two times, just to see if it helps you. I rely on my *Fifteen-Second TBI Routine* first thing in the morning when I wake up and my ravenous Beast starts feasting furiously on me. I bitch-slap intently and then segue into my TBI routine.

 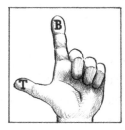 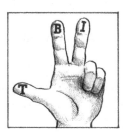

You can easily do it, too, in fifteen seconds or less. All you need are three fingers and your imagination. Spend five measly seconds apiece on the three tasks below:

1. **Thanks.** Raise your closed fist, and then extend your thumb to represent the letter T. Speak or think of something you can appreciate right now. It can be something real—"I appreciate this beautiful sunrise"— or farcical—"I am glad I don't need an iron lung to breathe."

2. **Bless.** Now extend your index finger as well, to signify the letter B. Think of an individual or group—living or dead—you wish to send healing or loving feelings to. Generate and send.

3. **Intend.** Then extend your middle finger to represent the letter I. Imagine one action you intend to undertake today. It can be anything from, "I am going to sit on the crapper for a long time" to "I shall start writing my first novel."

Do the Fifteen-Second TBI Routine as often as possible, at least once a day. To help you remember it, think of the acronym **TBI**, for *thanks, bless, intend.* Try it right now, and don't forget to include your thumb and fingers. TBI in fifteen seconds or less!

THANKS _____

_____

BLESS _____

_____

INTEND _____

_____

Naturally, The Beast will have something shitty to say about each TBI effort you make. Don't let this micro-slash surprise or annoy you. Bitch-slap the Beast.

At the beginning of this chapter, I urged you to read it, and I thank you if you did. I now hope you can catch those momentary silences in your shit storm and fill them with thoughts that feel *good-ish.* You'll be glad you did!

We have reached a turning point in *The Seven.* Your first four hacks focus entirely on the shit show in your head. Assuming you have actually delivered on your intention to make some changes, you first got good at calling out each thought-feeling micro-slash The Beast uses to diminish your life force. You grew insanely vigilant at bitch-slapping The Beast for every frickin' micro-slash. You deployed diversion techniques to cut down on the sheer volume of micro-slashing and bitch-slapping.

Now you're filling brief breaks in your shit storm—breaks *you* created, by the way—with intentional thoughts that kindle appreciation, blessings, or intent. Perhaps you even feel a twinge of hope that you might someday raise your emotional set point permanently to Neutral and beyond.

The first four hacks are *simple*—far simpler than psychotherapy, cognitive behavioral therapy, internal family systems, or conference room therapy for your twenty-two personality fragments. We have dramatically narrowed things down to your shit show, The Beast, a lot of bitch-slapping, some diversion, and a tiny touch of feeling good-ish. Even someone as depleted and miserable as you is getting juiced up for some serious bitch-slapping!

Now put this book down for a while—or lend it to a friend for a week—and practice your first four hacks. As you master them, your emotional set point will trend upward toward Neutral, and you will no longer be owned by The Beast. These four hacks alone will give you emotional freedom and renewed life force that—until recently—felt unattainable to you.

When you return, we shall turn our attention to the final three hacks, which will help the new and improved you deal with the craziness of your external world.

PART TWO

Hacking Your External World

"The foreign installation comes back, I assure you, but not as strong, and a process begins in which the fleeing of the flyer's mind becomes routine, until one day it flees permanently. A sad day indeed! That's the day when you have to rely on your own devices, which are nearly zero. There's no one to tell you what to do. There's no mind of foreign origin to dictate the imbecilities you're accustomed to."

Don Juan instructing Carlos Castaneda
in _The Active Side of Infinity_

Welcome to the Foam Pit

As you beat back The Beast and gain some control over your thoughts, you create an opening to make new choices to create a better life for yourself. Don't expect to fix everything in your life all at once—or ever, for that matter—but do expect to move your emotional set point upward, on a consistently more positive trend line as we move through the *Seven Life Hacks*.

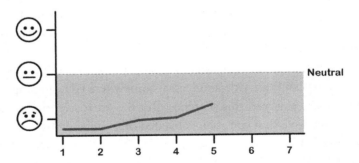

Our final three hacks equip you to cope with life outside your mental shit show: with other people, events, responsibilities, and your body. Before I unveil *Hack Five*, I need to conjure some appropriate context about life in our external world.

What I'm about to say is every bit as off-the-wall as what I've said about the source of your thoughts and how to improve them. So, do not expect me to insist love and compassion are the solutions to your life's shortcomings. "All you need is love" might work for some people, but not for folks suffering from chronic depression and anxiety. We need hacks to cope with the external shit show. So let's get started.

Why Are We Here?

First, a smidgeon of background discussion is necessary. If at any point it strikes you as completely irrelevant to relieving your misery, hang in there with me anyway. This is important, and it will consume only a few pages.

These pages are important because we must form a framework to support your choices and actions in daily life. The enduring question *"Why are we here?"* should be a reasonable starting point, yet it is fraught with difficulties. After centuries of careful consideration and analysis by clever minds in diverse civilizations, mankind is arguably more confused than ever by this simple question.

For starters, where exactly is "here" and who exactly are "we?" Yes, you probably are sitting on a seat somewhere you can pinpoint on a map as you read this sentence. But the great scientific minds among us agree that your seat is located on a globe whose equator rotates at 1,670 kilometers per hour (km/h) as it races around the sun at 107,000 km/h. That speed is sluggish, however, compared to the 720,000 km/h at which the Earth, sun and the rest of our solar system are hurtling through the galaxy. That's about 200 kilometers (120 miles) *per second*, yet your hairstyle is not even getting messed up.

Our all-important sun is only one of 100 billion or so stars in the Milky Way galaxy, which, in turn, is only one of 100 billion or so galaxies, all racing apart through vast, empty space at breakneck speeds. These 100 billion galaxies and billion-trillion stars, along with everything else in the universe supposedly originated from a single Big Bang within a spot smaller than a pinhead. Think about it. Unbelievable, right? It gets *much* weirder.

That empty space everything is racing through is not empty at all. It contains *dark matter*—a mysterious substance that emits or reflects no light and accounts for approximately 95 percent of the mass in the universe—and *dark energy*, both of which scientists cannot identify or explain.

The "matter" we can see, such as your chair and even your body, is composed of molecules, which, in turn, are comprised of atoms, which are 99.9999999999999 percent empty space. That's correct: in essence, you and I are empty space, and we don't know specifically what "empty space" is.

Why am I telling you this? I am trying to loosen whatever ideas you tenaciously grasp about "why we are here" by first introducing the possibility that we do not really understand what "we" are or where "here" actually is. Anyone who pays any attention to the claims and controversies of modern quantum theory will agree that our universe is much weirder and more unfathomable than previously suspected.

You'll recall that I asked to you join me (with no real proof) in selecting The Beast as an explanation for the source of your shitty thoughts. Whether or not The Beast is true, the concept of the Foreign Installation proved useful in restoring your life force by changing the tenor of your internal world. Shortly, I'll propose an answer to "why we are here" that will help you reset your expectations, judgments, and reactions in your external world and live a consistently better life.

Many of the scientific "facts" I presented above have emerged in the last hundred years or less, yet mankind has been trying to figure out "why we are here" for thousands of years. Curiously, most cultures believe human physical existence is part of a larger system that includes the continuation of individual consciousness in *non-physical environments* after death. Life on Earth, in most belief systems, is a testing ground where an individual's actions determine what happens to him or her after death. Perhaps you subscribe to one of them? Here are a few examples:

Linear systems, such as the Abrahamic traditions (Christianity, Judaism, Islam, Bahá'í Faith) essentially believe you get one shot at living a good life, and—upon your after-death judgment by a spiritual authority—you spend eternity on a plane of non-physical existence that reflects how deserving you are of reward or punishment. In a nutshell, each individual consciousness gets one shot on Earth to win eternal happiness. Picture yourself walking a tight rope in heavy winds. Your heart's every desire is on the other side, but below is the pit of hellfire. Step carefully! Oops, that's life!

Cyclical systems, such as Buddhism, Hinduism, Jainism, and Sikhism, generally believe humans receive unlimited chances to live a noble life and achieve enlightenment. Your actions in your most recent life determine what happens to you between lives and what situations you'll encounter when you reincarnate back into the physical realms. You stay stuck in this Karmic cycle until you finally learn all your lessons and evolve into an enlightened soul. Good luck getting off that carnival ride!

Newer views of spirituality also believe individual consciousness survives physical death, but they don't see each human life as a test. They instead see mankind's ultimate and inevitable evolution into super-human, Christ-like custodians of the physical universe. (For terrific examples of this perspective, see Ken Carey's *Starseed Transmissions* and Claire Heartsong's *Anna, Grandmother of Jesus*.)

There exist, of course, scores of other religions and theological traditions whose tenets I could oversimplify and misinterpret, such as the ancient Greek, Roman, Egyptian, African, and Norse systems of belief about "why we are here." My simple point, though, is that at least 80 percent of living humans believe in a non-physical afterlife and consider their current lives as a test of some sort. (If you are part of the 20 percent who do not believe in any afterlife or non-physical existence, just play pretend with me for a bit longer. Consider this a metaphorical discussion!)

Consider This Possibility

The "why we are here" explanation I find most compelling and useful for our goal of restoring your life force comes from the folks who claim to explore the after-death environment personally and extensively through out-of-body and similar trance states, and from those who channel information from entities that claim to inhabit the non-physical domains. Their detailed descriptions essentially depict physical existence as a *training ground for gaining control over one's thoughts and emotions.*

As an acceptable, if imperfect, metaphor, imagine the huge foam pit in a gymnastics gymnasium. As gymnasts learn a new skill, they perform repeatedly over a huge, foam-filled pit, which cushions their crooked landings and falls. They advance from the foam pit only after they develop enough skill to perform the new skill on their respective apparatus with low risk of injury. Likewise, humans stay in the physical realms until they gain control over their thoughts and emotions; then they move into a different arena.

Why do we need to control our thoughts and emotions? In this paradigm, the physical world we inhabit (which, remember, is 99.9999999999999 percent empty space) is the "densest" layer of a vast, multi-dimensional, vibrational universe with countless realities. Most of them are non-physical.

We see and experience only the physical layer we inhabit because our senses are tuned specifically to its *vibrational frequency*, much like a television is tuned to an individual station and ignores all the other existing audio-visual waves.

Throughout this multi-layered universe, individual thoughts are powerful creators of reality. They mold energies much like sculptors transform clay into fine art. A defining characteristic of each of these reality layers—both physical and non-physical—is how "thought-responsive" it is. That is, how quickly and easily do your individual thoughts and emotions manifest as reality?

The physical plane and nearby dense layers of reality—such as the so-called astral plane—are less thought-responsive. They're stable and constant (knock on wood), because they are *consensus thought realities*, created and sustained by mass consciousness, that is, the compatible thoughts and beliefs of many, many minds. Each individual thought is relatively less powerful and creative here because it is just a tiny fragment of the consensus thought reality.

In contrast, outer layers of the system are *non-consensus realities*. In these, your individual thoughts instantly and continuously create your perceptions and experiences. To ultimately gain admittance to those outer layers, ***each of us has to establish control over our mental and emotional gyrations.***

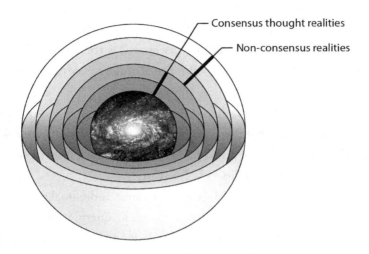

*The physical universe is the densest plane of
a multi-dimensional, thought-responsive universe.*

To make this concept easy to grasp, consider this depiction in *The Secret of the Soul* by noted author, teacher, and metaphysician, William Buhlman:

> Imagine a perfect world where your thoughts instantly create any reality you choose. Whatever your heart desires is suddenly made manifest before you....
> Imagine yourself in an ideal world where everyone is free to explore and develop their creative pursuits and experience their unlimited potential. Does this sound like heaven?
> Just think what an immature or undisciplined being could or would do in this ideal thought-responsive

world.... One undisciplined mind would wreak complete havoc, destroying the perfection of the subtle environments....

Now for a moment imagine what kind of educational environment would be the perfect training ground for this undisciplined mind.... What kind of lessons would effectively train this disruptive mind to coexist in the thought-responsive heavenly realms?

Welcome to the slowed-down molecular training ground of consciousness. Welcome to the dense training ground of matter, where focused thoughts are required in order to create and prosper. Welcome to the ideal environment where the young and undisciplined mind can learn by trial and error without contaminating the pure realm of spirit. Welcome to your life.

Can this be true? Who the hell knows! It certainly is no more outlandish than whichever paradigm most of us presently endorse about why we are here. In any event—just like The Beast—this paradigm can help restore your life force as painlessly as possible. Let's go with it for now. You can thank me later!

In a nutshell: we humans are relegated to physical existence because we are wholly unqualified to cavort in the outer layers of the multi-dimensional, thought-responsive, spiritual universe. We are in the bush league, the remedial class. We are the beginners, the trainees, the misfits. Our minds are drunken monkeys. We are *constrained by molecular and energetic density*, so our errant thoughts don't immediately manifest chaos all around us. We are stuck in the proverbial foam pit of our magnificent, multi-dimensional universe.

What does any of this have to do with restoring your life force? In a manner similar to using the metaphor of The Beast to explain your inner world and create a coping strategy for your mental shit show, we'll use the concept of being mired in the lowest, densest layer of consciousness to generate a coping strategy for preserving your life force as you engage with your external existence. This is going to be fun!

Mayhem with the Misfits

Let me briefly make my case that we are gyrating in the foam pit of our multi-dimensional universe, and our predominant theme is *Mayhem with the Misfits*.

Picture a preschool or kindergarten class of thirty energetic youngsters, running around and enjoying being with each other. Finger painting is next on the agenda, and the teacher lays out a white poster board for each student, along with several large pots of red, blue, green, yellow and black finger paints. Suddenly the teacher's intestines erupt and she rushes off to the restroom, leaving the kiddies unsupervised. One thing leads to another, and she's gone from the class for thirty minutes or so. What manner of scene does she return to? Order and serenity? Of course not! She returns to mayhem! Wildlings running around, splashing paint on the walls, desks, themselves and each other. A couple of paint-splattered little girls in pretty dresses, crying in the corner. One or two parentified kids trying vainly to establish order. In short, she encounters a microcosm of human life!

I picked just a handful of headlines from daily news feeds to illustrate how whacked-out our foam-pit world is. Skim these headlines for a small sample of the mayhem we see on Earth every day:

- Oregon daycare owner gets 21 years for drugging kids, leaving them to go tanning.
- Woman who killed beau in YouTube stunt gets 180 days in jail.
- World's largest collection of garbage is now twice the size of Texas.
- I'm the girl who clawed her own eyes out. This is my story.
- Record numbers of college students are seeking treatment for depression and anxiety—but schools can't keep up.
- Naked gunman kills 4 in Waffle House shooting, remains at large.
- German nurse who murdered 87 patients given life sentence.
- DNA test reveals fertility doctor used own sperm to impregnate patient.
- Pennsylvania man steals mom's car before backing over her and fleeing scene, police say.
- 24.9 million persons trapped in modern-day slavery
- Indonesian woman swallowed whole by 23-foot python
- Mississippi man killed wife and friends after they wouldn't let him drive drunk, police say.

- Catholic priests abused 1,000 kids in Pennsylvania, report says.
- My fiancé postponed our wedding, secretly bought a house—and told me I could pay rent.

I could go on and on with this, but you see the point, right? Perhaps you retort that most of the world's population flows through the day in an orderly fashion, and these headlines are eye-popping because they are so unusual. Fair enough, but bear in mind that in the last century alone, humans murdered about 200 million members of their own species through war, famine, and oppression. (For gruesome details, check out http://necrometrics. com/all20c.htm.) It is impossible to picture that many people, let alone imagining their suffering and the mayhem that caused it.

Still not convinced our dominant planetary theme is Mayhem with the Misfits? We humans are wreaking havoc on other members of the animal kingdom, not just upon ourselves. According to the World Wildlife Fund, *humans have wiped out about half the world's wild animals since 1970*—that's less than one human lifetime! Let's not even talk about the percentage of wild animals obliterated before 1970.

Journalist Elizabeth Kolbert won a Pulitzer Prize for her 2014 book, *The Sixth Extinction: An Unnatural History,* which predicts mankind will exterminate twenty to fifty percent of *all flora and fauna species* by the end of this century.

Well, that's enough effort to promote the notion that Earth is the remedial training ground for human consciousness, and our dominant theme, *Mayhem with the Misfits,* is at least as defensible as whatever concepts most of us currently endorse.

I can't blame you if you're stubbornly resisting this idea. First, I informed you that an invisible, inorganic Beast incessantly force-feeds you shitty thoughts so it can devour your life force, and now I assert that you're ensconced for countless lifetimes in a dense vibrational foam pit with a bunch of Misfits hell-bent on Mayhem. Yikes, no wonder you're depressed and/or anxious!

Believe it or not, accepting this theme will help you restore and retain your life force. Here is how endorsing *Mayhem with the Misfits* can reset your expectations and reactions in your external world and help you feel immediate relief:

- You realize you're right where you need to be. You definitely do not have control of your thoughts; am I right? You belong here in the foam pit to minimize the existential damage caused by your drunken-monkey thinking.

- Guess what? Pretty much everyone else you encounter in daily life is here for the same reason you are: They suck at controlling their thoughts. They might be richer, prettier, smarter, healthier, more athletic, and more popular than you, but, hey, they are stuck in the foam pit too!

- Being burdened with a ravenous Beast might mean you are an *advanced* player on this foam pit level of our multi-dimensional reality. Maybe you're earning extra points by bearing the Beast!

- You're now vigorously bitch-slapping The Beast all the live-long day, which is a major step towards controlling your thoughts and emotions and graduating to a lovelier level of existence. This is good!

- If you kill yourself now, you'll probably end up right back on this level in your next life, dealing with the Misfits and their Mayhem, so you might as well hang around and finish this episode of your personal series.
- You no longer need to become upset when shit happens in your daily life. What can you expect from the Misfits, but Mayhem? Nothing anyone does can ever surprise you or knock you off center. You'll simply raise your eyebrows, shrug your shoulders, and say, "Mayhem… with the Misfits…"
- Instead of expecting everything in life to go your way and getting annoyed and angry when things go awry, you can be truly appreciative when any endeavor turns out half as well as you hoped. Take any positive outcome as a sign that you just made a small step toward reaching another level.

Just to be sure you are grokking the value of *Mayhem with the Misfits*, let's construct a couple of examples.

Imagine you finally bought the fabulous new car you have been saving for over many months. You wash and wax it till it gleams, and you proudly transport your pals to a fantastic concert. When you return to the parking lot after the show, you realize some asshole has dragged his key along the length of your car, inscribing a long, jagged scratch across the shiny red finish.

Previously, you would have had a shit-fit, ranted and raged, and been unable to stop thinking about the injustice of life. Or maybe you would have been furious with yourself for "manifesting" such a shitty reality. Now, with your wisdom of accepting life in the foam pit, you simply raise your eyebrows, shrug your shoulders, mumble, "Mayhem… with the frigging Misfits," and get on with your evening.

As another surprisingly common example, imagine you come home early from a stressful day of work, feeling feverish, and trudge into your bedroom to find your beloved mate enthusiastically fornicating with your best friend. Holy crap! Previously, you would flip out and—perhaps depending on your gender—either head for your gun cabinet or to the kitchen pantry to binge on chocolate. Now, you are unshaken. What can you expect from Misfits? You breezily snap a couple of pics of the naked fuckers and post them to your social media accounts.

I could do this all day, but it is your turn to write one memorable *Mayhem with the Misfits* example from your own experience in the foam pit:

_____

_____

_____

_____

_____

_____

_____

Now you possess a potent paradigm for dealing with the external shit storms that invade your daily life. Let's drill down to specific ways to cope with the people in your life who drain your life force. Move on to *Hack Five*!

Hack Five: U Do U

Hack Five: U Do U helps you cope with the people in your life, especially the Misfits with their Mayhem. Brace yourself—this is our most massive hack. It spans two chapters. By the end of this first chapter, you'll own these skills:

1. How to "be the boss of you" by repeatedly asking and answering *The Question,* day in and day out.
2. How to respond to Shit Slingers who assault you verbally.
3. How to avoid being pulled into situations that drain your life force.

The Boss of You

Given that you're still reading this book, I believe you've made two crucial changes to your present awareness. First, you're reflexively vigilant at monitoring your life force and instantly aware when it's attacked by The Beast. Second, you're bitch-slapping The Beast into moments of submission and silence. If so, you know you truly do exist apart from your shit-storm of shitty thoughts, and you are amassing willpower to determine how you will spend your time in this foam pit of our multi-dimensional universe.

Hack Five: U Do U comes into play because you've used the first four hacks to win back some control over your life and now, Skipper, you have to own it. As I promised in the very beginning, the *Dominated* is now becoming the *Dominator*. Congratulations, you are the new boss of you!

The Question

Being the "boss of you" is surprisingly straightforward. You merely have to ask, answer, and act on one simple question over and over and over. I am paraphrasing a vital question presented in *Conversations with God* by Neale Donald Walsch, so you could say it comes straight from God to you (via Neale and me). As you deal with the daily Mayhem of the Misfits and other wacky themes in the foam pit of our multi-dimensional universe, calmly and repeatedly ask yourself The Question: ***Who (or how) do I choose to be in relation to this?***

In other words, how do I choose to respond (if at all), right now, to my immediate situation? How will I represent myself and express what I stand for?

Asking The Question and waiting for your personal answer during the drama of daily life gives you important benefits:

1. The Question reminds you that *you are the boss of you*. You might suck at controlling your thoughts, but you still get to choose how you speak and act! The Beast

undoubtedly will interject a shitty answer for you, but you are well-prepared to bitch-slap it away.

2. Asking The Question creates a momentary pause that blocks reflexive emotional reactions and gives you time to ponder whether you even want to participate in the immediate flavor of Mayhem before you.

3. Third, over time, you'll develop an amazing sense of personal freedom by asking and answering The Question honestly. Amazing life changes are in store for you.

Full disclosure: I am making this sound easy, but it is not, at least initially. You haven't been asking and answering this question with any regularity, have you? If you had, you would not be depressed or anxious. You would be living your life with a sense of purpose and control. As it is, The Beast has been torturing you with fearful and threatening thoughts about failure and loss and inadequacy, so you've been too inundated with shit to ask yourself *who you really want to be in each moment* of your life.

Let's dream up a couple of examples, starting with a simple one. Imagine you are about to unload a cart full of grocery bags into the trunk of your car on a beautiful day. The motor of the delivery truck parked next to you is running and the driver is sitting behind the wheel, looking at his phone, with the windows open. His truck's huge tailpipe is pumping smelly, noxious gas right into your face. You wonder, "Why is this knucklehead letting his truck pollute the atmosphere, waste fuel, and blow toxic gas in my face?"

You ask yourself The Question. "How do I want to respond to this?" You immediately see several options: You can ask him to turn off his engine. You can wait a short distance out of range for a few moments to see if he leaves. Or you can hold your breath and quickly unload the groceries, muttering to yourself as you go.

What *should* you do? I don't know and don't care—it is none of my business. The point is, you have to ask, answer, and act upon The Question, all day, every day. How do *you* choose to respond to this situation? Maybe The Beast is calling you names for not insulting the driver, or maybe you want to say something to him, but you are afraid of confrontation.

Hack Five says you get to decide and you merely have to *own* whatever decision you make, without regret or self-recrimination— and without listening to your damn Beast. In the long run, most of your daily life does not matter, but your life force depends on your making an endless stream of decisions, owning them, and acting on them.

For our second example, imagine you have saved for many months to purchase a once-in-a-lifetime luxury cruise through the Mediterranean with your best friend. Unfortunately, your BFF turns out to be a lousy travel companion in every way. She whines and complains about every little travel inconvenience, she's a slob in the stateroom, she's insufferable at the dinner table, and she keeps trying to steal your dates at the nightclub. In the old days, you would have suffered silently for days, until you finally freaked out, blew your top at her, sulked for the rest of the trip, and maybe even terminated your friendship.

Now, armed with *Hack Five*, you ask yourself The Question at the first sign of mini-mayhem. "Who do I choose to be in relation to this petty tyrant?"

At the first sign of trouble, you can say something like, "Hey, we will have a lot more fun on this vacay if we wisecrack instead of complaining about these inevitable inconveniences. Okay with you?" Or, "Jeez, I love the way you so effortlessly decorated our entire cabin with your dirty laundry! Can you put your clothes in this hamper here, or maybe chuck them out the porthole?"

I bet you don't like this idea one bit, do you? Let's face it, you *are* too nice. We already know that. You don't like to hurt other people's feelings, and you avoid interpersonal conflict. As a result, you let your own feelings get hurt, time and time again. *Absorbing "the hit" repeatedly is a lot like accepting every micro-cut from The Beast: Both destroy your life force.*

So, ask The Question, answer it, and take the action that's required by your answer. Start with small situations and you will inexorably build up sufficient life force to take control of the bigger issues that plague you.

As the first part of *Hack Five: U Do U*, you ask yourself The Question ("Who do I choose to be, right now, in response to this?") about any aspect of your life at any time—your job, your school, your home, your family, your friends, your hobbies, your health, or your finances. Be on the lookout for those issues that drain your life force the most, typically where you feel trapped or hopeless. Because you are stuck with the rest of us in the foam pit of Mayhem, I doubt you'll succeed at effortlessly improving every situation. But you will move steadily and incrementally in the direction of *Who You Want to Be.*

As a more compelling example, let's imagine you hate your job, and The Beast is saying you have no options for a better situation. You are a devout vegan working 12-hour days scraping cattle bones in a meat-packing plant because it's the only job in your small town that pays enough money to support your infirm parents, your disabled spouse, and your six special-needs foster kids. You feel stuck in this depressing situation, and your Beast is having a field day with it. You were suicidal, but now you are bitch-slapping The Beast relentlessly and clinging to the slight improvement in your life force. You are ready to ask yourself, "Who do I choose to be in relation to this shitty situation?"

Sorry, but the price of this book cannot buy you an easy answer to daunting problems that plague you. However, the *U Do U Hack* creates a whiteboard for you to sketch out an expanded view of possibilities. You list as many options as you can think of, you tell The Beast to shut up when it interferes, and you consider at your leisure which of these options best represents who you will become.

It is your life, and ultimately *your only real obligation is to choose something that bolsters your life force and to act on it.* It is far better you disappoint other people with your choices than be so miserable trying to please everyone that you want to die.

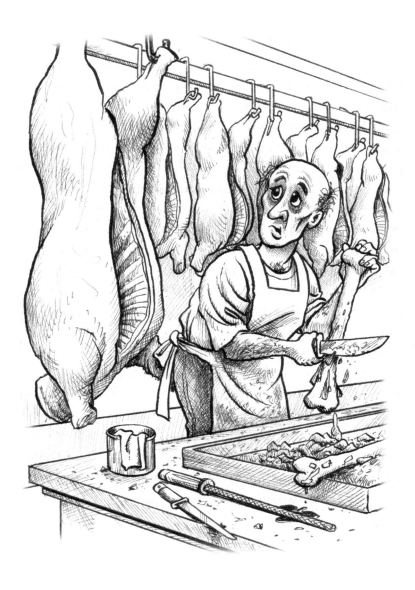

Let's consider a few options for our depressing example of the long-suffering vegan working in the meat-packing plant, bearing in mind that your Beast's opinion is irrelevant:

1. Work toward a job at the plant that gets you off the meat-cutting line, such as delivery driver or an office job.

2. Run away and let your relatives fend for themselves.

3. Accept that animals are part of the food chain and vigorously express your inner butcher.

4. Move everyone to a bigger town, wait tables at a vegan restaurant, and supplement your income by driving for Uber and pet-sitting for Rover.com.

5. Study online courses at night to learn new skills that offer a chance for a better job.

6. Supplement your income by starting a YouTube channel, *Travails of the Vegan Meat Packer*, potentially leading to your own reality show on cable TV.

There are many other possibilities, of course. Only you can know the best answer for you at any given time, the one that increases the flow of your life force and moves your emotional set point closer to Neutral. Be willing to consider any fresh idea that delivers a little jolt of life force.

The first, and main, point of *Hack Five* is this: In the absence of The Beast running and ruining your life, you have the bona fide opportunity to *be the boss of you*. Asking and answering The Question ("Who do I choose to be in relation to this situation?") many times each day is the ideal way to begin the process. Start with simple issues in the present moment, and gradually move to the larger, more complex issues that plague you.

... Five Years from Now

A word of caution: Asking and answering The Question without adequate thought of potential consequences can yield short-term solutions for long-term problems, which might lead to trouble.

For example, imagine you are sitting in your molecular biophysics class, straining to keep your eyes open as your ancient professor, speaking English as her third language, drones on unintelligibly. You need to ace this class to have any hope of getting into medical school and becoming a successful brain surgeon like dear old Dad. You ask The Question, "Who do I want to be in relation to this old fart at the front of the room, to my dad, to brain surgery in general?"

The answer comes back immediately. "Screw this! I don't want to be a brain surgeon. I wanna play my guitar full-time and make a living as a street musician in Haight-Ashbury!" So, off you go, full of zest for life! Unfortunately, in a few months you might ask yourself The Question, "Who do I want to be in relation to the fact that I have no money and nowhere to live?"

The Question is a loaded bazooka that can seriously blow stuff up. Be careful where you point it. It's easy and less risky to quickly answer The Question when dealing with the immediate shit show around you—you get a flat tire, your kids are bickering, your waitress sucks, your boss criticizes you, your best friend throws up on you, and so on.

For questions potentially having longer-term repercussions—"Should I tell my boss he's a whack job?" or "Should I cheat on my spouse?" or "Should I drop out of school?"—it is imperative to consider the long term implications.

I suggest tagging one simple phrase to the end of The Question: "… five years from now." If our bored college student above asks, "Who do I want to be in relation to this lousy professor… five years from now?" the subsequent internal dialogue and decision will hopefully be more informed and less impulsive.

What if your answer to The (expanded) Question still tells you to blow shit up? Should you? Well, yes, maybe you should! Remember, you are so depressed or anxious you wish you were dead; the downside cannot be all that significant. Maybe you need some *really* big changes in your life. I call this the Nuclear Option and we'll discuss it more in *Hack Six*. Please don't blow up anything huge until you finish this book, OK?

In the meantime, practice asking and answering The Question—with and without the five-year clause—as often as you can. The brief time required to dream up your answer creates a buffer that eliminates your impulsive reaction to the Mayhem in the foam pit and frees you to choose a response that preserves and strengthens your life force.

We invested a solid ten pages into The Question. It is that important. Tell me, who do you choose to be in relation to The Question suggestion? Will you start using it? It is fine with me if you shut this book for a couple of days while you figure that out. Then rejoin me for phase two of *Hack Five: U Do*.

Shit Slingers

Phase two helps you cope specifically with people who contribute negatively to the shit show in your head. I call them "Shit Slingers," but you might prefer a different moniker, such as control freaks, assholes, dirtbags, petty tyrants, or narcissistic psychopaths. Their presence in your life is every bit as toxic as The Beast.

By my definition, *Shit Slingers are those who deplete your life force.* That's it. Anyone whose presence or behavior diminishes your life force is your personal Shit Slinger. An individual might be popular, honored, or even revered by other people, but if his or her effect on you is negative, you are dealing with a Shit Slinger, and you'll have to proceed accordingly.

I could go on about who these people are and how they treat others, but you already recognize the Shit Slingers in your life, don't you? I bet you have at least one who comes immediately to mind.

But wait, don't some apparent Shit Slingers have your best intentions at heart? Don't they mean well? Yes, of course, some do.

Let's say you're a teenager whose parents are freaked because you are flunking out of high school, hanging out with gang members, smoking dope before breakfast, and wearing lowrider pants that show six inches of butt crack.

Or, you are an unemployed husband with two young kids. Your wife is furious with you for playing video games on the sofa all day and night, while she works long hours and does all the mothering and housekeeping. Don't these people have a right to sling some serious shit at you, hoping to save you from yourself?

Well, yes, indeed they do. But how has that been working for you all? Not great, I bet. Nobody can pull you out of your shitty situation but yourself, and you need to renew your life force to generate enough energy to move you in a better direction.

If we can silence The Beast and the Shit Slingers long enough for you to get skilled at asking and answering The Question, you might build enough enthusiasm for this life that you will hang around and participate in a meaningful way.

After you use one of the techniques described below to stabilize your life force, I suggest telling the well-meaning person in your life how you are using *The Seven Life Hacks* to get better.

Dealing with Shit Slingers

Your skill at *Hack One: The Micro-Slash Hack* has prepared you for dealing with Shit Slingers. You'll easily recognize every shit sling the instant it flies at you, and you'll be ready to respond before the shit sticks and further diminishes your depleted life force.

However, managing Shit Slingers is more complicated than bitch-slapping The Beast because the Slingers, as your parents, teachers, bosses, spouses, friends, or partners, often have power over your life circumstances. Responding to a shit-sling with "blow it out your ass" could have serious repercussions. As an alternative to bitch-slapping, I offer you three additional techniques:

- Dodge
- Smack-back
- Broken Record

The Dodge

The Dodge is the easiest technique. When you sense some shit winging your way, you simply dodge out of the way and ignore it. It does not diminish your life force.

The secret to a successful dodge lies in the second of Don Miguel Ruiz's *Four Agreements:* "Don't take anything personally." You conclude the nastiness has little to do with you; it's the Slinger's reaction to his or her own internal Beastly battle. So, you merely nod slightly or raise your eyebrows to acknowledge that the Slinger is dealing with his or her own emotional poison, and you let the shit fly on by. You are Teflon, baby!

The Dodge is most useful for smaller shit-slings. For example, on a lunch date your friend greets you with, "Gee, you look tired!" [small ouch]. Before reading this book, you probably thought, "Do I? Oh, I must look like crap. I'd better rush to the restroom and freshen up!" Now, in your testy, bitch-slapping mode, you might be tempted to retort, "Oh yeah? Well, if I had a face like yours, I'd shave my ass and walk backward!" But hey, there's no good reason to bring a firearm to a fiddle-sticks fight, so now you simply *dodge* the remark (with raised eyebrows) and watch it ease on into the ether. In other words, don't sweat the small shit, and don't let it diminish your life force.

The Smack-back

Unfortunately, it isn't *all* small shit. Inevitably, you get hit with a load of crap that is too massive to dodge. Whenever you feel a Slinger's words or actions inflicting damage to your life force, it's time to abandon the Dodge and unleash the Smack-back. In essence, you smack the emotional poison—the turd—right back at them before it can stick to you and diminish your life force.

What should you say? Frankly, it does not matter, as *long as your life force is immediately restored.* Your response is similar to how you handle The Beast. There is no need to discuss, argue, reason, cajole, or coddle. Communicate—to them and to yourself—that you will not be intimidated or diminished. It could be as simple as saying, "Ooh, that was nasty!" or "That's not how I see it." Or it could be as vicious as, "Tell me, does your anus ever get jealous of the *crap* that comes out of your mouth?"

Decide how nasty and vitriolic you must be to immediately restore your life force to whatever level it was before the verbal feces smacked into your face. Let's do a little exercise to illustrate this. Suppose you're a woman and one of your best friends says, "Honey, I know I was a bridesmaid at your wedding and you helped me plan mine and shop for my dress, but unfortunately my fiancé has such a big family that I can't invite you to my ceremony. I still have a seat for you at table 19 at my reception, but you won't be able to bring a guest." Ouch, do you feel the sudden drop in your life force? Of course you do!

In the old days, you would have answered meekly, "Oh, I'm so sorry to see you under such pressure. It's OK, honey, no problem, I understand completely." In other words, "I am your rug. Please, walk all over me." And off you'd slink with your diminished, feeble life force.

But now you are a bitch-slapping Beast slayer, and you immediately recognize the splat of a Shit Slinger. You are ready for action. You have the presence of mind to ask yourself The Question: Who do you want to be in relation to this Shit Slinger? The key issue is, how nasty should your reply be?

Because you're habitually bitch-slapping The Beast so aggressively, you will be tempted to respond cuttingly. "Oh, no biggie, honey. I have to pass on your wedding, anyway. My annual mammogram is scheduled that day, and I'd just *hate* to miss it!" OK, not bad, that's an improvement. Is your life force restored to its level prior to the shit-sling?

That's the goal of the Smack-back: to instantly neutralize the hit to your life force. I call this technique the Smack-back, not the Ace or the Kill Shot, because you don't want to escalate the shit slinging; you just want to even things up and keep the ball in play, so to speak.

A more thoughtful response might be, "Wow, that really hurts my feelings. I am so disappointed. I thought I was your best friend, and you would insist on sharing your special time with me. I guess I overestimated our friendship." Bingo, life force restored!

I like this more measured approach because it is sincere and it keeps the door open for further communication and connection. Despite mixing metaphors, let's call this the High Road Smack-back. Whenever possible, use your Smack-backs to *tell your highest truth without spite or rancor.* With a bit of practice, you can take the high road and still regain your lost life force immediately.

Let's try another example. You're on an expensive dinner date with your wife/girlfriend, and you comment that your entree is overcooked. She says, "*Jesus*, do you have to complain about everything? You're just like your father. Why can't you just enjoy the meal?" Ouch, that's some serious crapola winging your way! When you were chronically depressed, you probably would have said nothing in reply and simply sulked for the remainder of the meal. Now, as a skilled bitch-slapper, your reflexive response might be, "You are so right! Why am I complaining? It's still a lot better than everything you've ever cooked!"

Because it restored your life force, this is an acceptable Smack-back, but it's not a great one. The High Road approach is more like, "Ouch, that hurt. I feel criticized for simply commenting on my food." This Smack-back does not escalate. It is neutral, but hopefully it still preserves your life force.

Because you are too nice a person, you might be tempted to add, "Are you mad at me for something else?" I don't recommend this, because it draws attention away from the fact that she just slung shit at you while you are already dealing with an overcooked entree, and you would have appreciated a little sympathy.

She replies, "Well, you always complain about everything." More shit. Your bitch-slapping Smack-back: "Anyone who spends an evening with you will have a lot to complain about!" Your High Road Smack-back: "Hmmm, that's two absolutes, 'always' and 'everything.' I have the feeling you don't like me very much." The High Road Smack-back lets you stand your ground without escalating the conflict. You can do this indefinitely, and your life force will be preserved.

The High Road Smack-back immediately informs Shit Slingers that they cannot inflict their emotional poison upon you. Oh, they will continue to try, and you will continue to Smack-back, until they finally get the message. With a bit of practice, smacking-back at Shit Slingers can be fun, even invigorating.

The Broken Record

Sometimes, though, smacking-back with Shit Slingers gets exhausting. Much like The Beast, some Slingers will attack you relentlessly. When you find your Smack-backs getting weaker and your life force diminishing, you can always fall back on the Broken Record technique.

The Broken Record involves repeating the same phrase over and over again until the Shit Slinger gives up. If you like, you can pick two or three personal favorites and repeat them. Deliver them with a tone of finality that strengthens your life force. It's that simple. Here are a few examples.

- "I'm finished talking about this."
- "That's not how I see it."
- "I need to think about that."
- "Let's agree to disagree."
- "Ow, that hurt my feelings."
- "That's my business."
- "Stay in your lane!"
- "Let's change the subject."
- "Hey, you do you!"
- Yours:_____
- Yours:_____

Which phrase you select to repeat like a broken record is immaterial. What does matter is your state of mind, which must become every bit as relentless as the Shit Slingers'. Believe me, after a bit of practice, the Smack-back and Broken Record techniques become as reflexive and effective at preserving your life force as bitch-slapping.

Now, take a minute and pick one of the main Shit Slingers in your life. Write a typical shitty comment they sling at you, and then dream up a decent Smack-back, a High Road Smack-back, and a Broken Record response. If you enjoy this, grab a separate piece of paper and write responses to all the Shit Slingers you deal with daily.

Shit Slinger: _____

_____

_____

Smack-back: _____

_____

_____

High Road Smack-back:_____

_____

_____

Broken Record: _____

_____

_____

What Others Think of You

Perhaps you resist the idea of responding assertively to Shit Slingers. You fear your remarks might upset them, might make them judge you harshly, might even make them reject you and not be your friend/lover/spouse/partner/parent/etc. any longer.

Do you worry more or less continuously about what other people think of you? This fear is a potent weapon The Beast wields to create and sustain your anxiety and depression. The Beast taunts you with thoughts of how others might dislike your words, actions, appearance, or mere presence. Are you aware of this constant, nagging concern in the back of your mind? Tell me, do you think happy, productive people worry a great deal about what others think of them? Nah, they don't.

You'll recall at the beginning of this book I required your willingness to become a different person. You took a huge step when you agreed to recognize harmful thoughts and to bitch-slap The Beast relentlessly. I bet you're getting pretty good at it!

Now I'm compelling you to shift your background attention from worrying constantly about what people might think of you, toward a *vigilant recognition of how the words and actions of others impact your life force in every moment.* Safeguarding your life force must become the vital concern that drives how you interact with people.

As an aside, let me point out that fretting about what others might think is idiotic anyway. Most people have no control the Beast-driven shit shows in their heads. The critical thoughts they express about you stem from negativity The Beast is using to diminish their life force. Who cares what they think?

You will love the freedom that comes from honoring the old adage: *"What others think about me is none of my business."*

From this moment on, you are going to implement the same vigilance towards Shit Slingers that you apply to micro-slashes from The Beast. You are instantly going to recognize each hit and immediately apply a Dodge, Smack-back, High Road Smack-back, or Broken Record technique to recover your life force, regardless of what anyone thinks about it.

This might be a good time to close the book and spend a day or two thinking about the second element of *Hack Five: U Do U*: dealing with Shit Slingers who attack you verbally. Get your creative juices flowing, and have fun with it!

Not My Monkey

Learning to cope with Shit Slingers helps you preserve your life force from verbal attacks. Now we'll protect you from people *trying to control you and your actions.*

As a prelim to hacking your external world, I described the dominant theme of our material world as *Mayhem with the Misfits.* The third aspect of *Hack Five: U Do U* helps you allow the Misfits to do as they shall, without getting sucked into situations that drain your life force.

Do you sometimes comply with requests you definitely don't want to do? For example, in your senior year of high school, your best friend says, "Bro, you know I lost my driver's license from that dumb DUI, and I need to you drive me and Zoey around tonight for her school dance. You got a big back seat that we can put to good use!"

Or maybe your middle-aged coworker says, "I need you to take my two dogs and three cats this weekend because my new boyfriend is visiting from out of town and he's allergic."

Or imagine you're at dinner with two good friends in your senior-living dining room and a staff member stops by and says, "Can I seat poor Ms. Ruthie with you from now on? No one else will sit with her anymore." In each of these situations, you cringe when the request is made, yet you acquiesce because you feel obligated. Have you noticed how your life force takes a hit when you say OK, and diminishes still more as the event unfolds?

If you weren't depressed or anxious, we might agree it's OK to put up with the bullshit. After all, life is full of it. However, restoring your life force is our sole concern, and this is an opportunity to preserve our meager but precious gains. *You are growing skilled at recognizing when your life force is being threatened*, so you can easily sense when a request or a demand is potentially diminishing.

What to do? After all, you have not been verbally attacked; you've just been asked for a favor. It would be impolite to say no. What if you want a return favor in the near future? You always consider these thoughts when asked to do something you don't want to do. Then you comply to the detriment of your life force, right? Not anymore!

Recall at the beginning of *Hack Five: U Do U*, you learned to ask and answer The Question, **"Who/how do I choose to be in relation to this?"** Have you been working on that? I sincerely hope you are getting the hang of it.

Now we are going to expand the question. Ask yourself, *"Is this my circus, is this my monkey?"* If you decide you don't want the circus or the monkey—the fornicators in your back seat, the dogs and cats in your home, or unpopular Ms. Ruthie at your dinner table—just shake your head slowly and say, "not my circus, not my monkey." Then move along with your vital life force undiminished. You'll be amazed at how much more free time you'll have when you stop letting Misfits throw *their* monkeys onto *your* back.

Aren't you being selfish? Why, yes, you are. You are selfishly increasing and preserving your life force. If you sense that a requested action will actually increase your life force, then accept immediately, of course. If not, you must decline. When, in the coming times, your emotional set point stays firmly above Neutral, you'll be able to accept the occasional monkey on your back. For now, practice saying, however softly, "not my circus, not my monkey."

Relationship Circus

You'll probably encounter the most nettlesome shit-slinging and circus monkeys in your closest personal relationships. Some of your friends and family members take your feelings for granted as they obsess about the potential judgments of strangers. As a result, those closest to you say and do shitty, unfiltered things that hurt you, while walking on eggshells around other people. This is weird and ironic because, of course, *you* are most vulnerable to the words and actions of those closest to you. That's why some of the worst Shit Slingers are the very people you really care about disappointing.

For example, imagine you recently fell into an exciting new romance. You're cautiously optimistic that this young relationship can actually endure, and you start to believe you'll be happy at long last.

Suddenly, though, your new lover becomes irrationally jealous about your existing friendships and starts demanding that you cut them off. You are ordered to text your whereabouts continually, with real-time pics proving you are not with former lovers. As you grow more and more isolated, you feel increasingly anxious and afraid.

Oddly, you are not anxious about losing all your friends. Instead, you obsess about upsetting the narcissistic psychopath whose unjustified jealousy is sucking all the air out of the relationship.

What to do? You already know. You have two main hacks to unleash: bitch-slapping and asking/answering The Question.

First, realize The Beast is using your new lover as a potent theme to create highly-charged, shitty thoughts to rain down on you. This dysfunctional relationship is good for The Beast, so it's likely to give you lots of reasons to continue your unhappy romance. Oh, your lover is just insecure, suffers from the same anxiety as you, has been hurt before, has trouble trusting people, but maybe it can all be different with you. By now, perhaps you realize that even these supposedly hopeful thoughts feel shitty and are draining your precious life force.

Bitch-slap aggressively! Remember, the *content* of shitty thoughts is irrelevant. Worrying about what your lover thinks feels shitty. If it feels shitty, bitch-slap!

Next, ask yourself The Question: "How do I want to be in relation to an insanely jealous lover? Do I really want this monkey on my back?" If you are really strung out over this petty tyrant, you'd better face yourself in the mirror while you ask and answer.

Most likely, your honest answer to The Question will be stark enough to clear your head and help you side-step toxic relationships. If for some inane reason, you insist on hanging in there with your insanely jealous lover, you'll have to dodge, smack-back, and throw-down monkeys all the live-long day. It *is* your circus, it *is* your monkey!

Describe your most dysfunctional personal relationship:

_____

_____

_____

_____

_____

Now, answer The Question about this relationship:

_____

_____

_____

_____

_____

At this point in *Hack Five*, you're well-armed with powerful hacks to overcome external threats to your life force, as they occur:

- You ask and answer The Question to *be the boss of you.*
- You counter verbal attacks from Shit Slingers with your Dodge, Smack-back, and Broken Record techniques.
- You avoid getting sucked into the Mayhem by retorting, "not my circus, not my monkey."

Now, before we can move on to *Hack Six: The Daily Grind*, we must master the inevitable side effect of Hack Five, a disconcerting feeling of disconnection from our fellow humans.

Staying Connected

We're still discussing *Hack Five: U Do U*, but we're shifting gears a bit. In this chapter, you'll gain useful hacks to keep you from falling into the desolate void of complete disconnection from the human drama.

Human Folly

Repeatedly asking and answering The Question and subsequently repudiating the Misfits' monkeys—as we just discussed—will inevitably create a mood of detachment. We remain *in* the Mayhem but not *of* it, so to speak. The idiotic chaos around us is no longer our circus to the extent it once was. You might look at the daily machinations of your world and think, "Even if this does not rise to the level of Mayhem, it sure seems like utter folly."

For example, you're attending the lavish fortieth birthday bash of an old friend at an elegant Four Seasons ballroom. You are showcasing your best cocktail dress and five-inch heels that mangle your feet. You've had plenty to eat and drink, and you are starting to sag, physically and mentally. This is an adults-only affair, but a self-absorbed couple, whom you just met tonight, have brought their rowdy three-year-old twins. The rascals are zooming around the ballroom like miniature dervishes high on ayahuasca. Their slightly drunk mom leans over to you and says, "Honey, would you mind keeping an eye on little Travis and Tammy so my husband and I can go out to the parking lot and smoke some ganja?"

OK, maybe that's not Mayhem, but it easily rises to the level of folly, does it not? So, you shake your head calmly and say... what? "Not my circus, not my monkey!"

Controlled Folly

As the feckless folly of our fellow humans becomes increasingly apparent, their efforts to pull you into their daily dramas become less effective. The good news is, your *Hack Five* skills reduce the folly's negative impact on your life force. *The potential danger, though, is your becoming even more disengaged from life and disconnected from others than you were back on page one.* You might be less depressed and anxious, but you're still mired in an existential "Who gives a shit?" You feel like an astronaut untethered from the space station and floating free into the great void. What to do?

The best answer I've found comes from anthropologist Carlos Castaneda, the amazing guy who gave us the Foreign Installation presented in part one of this book. His mentor, Don Juan, advised Carlos to join his fellow men in the midst of their folly, but to *control his own folly.*[9] The act and habit of controlling his folly helped Carlos accumulate personal power for the development of a sorcerer's will. In our case, controlling our folly lets us join other folks in the midst of their folly while preserving our life force.

Hack Five: U Do U already gives you most of the tools needed to practice *controlled folly* in your daily life. You reflexively ask The Question, you forcefully smack-back at Shit Slingers, and you flamboyantly fling monkeys off your back. You are unhooking from the folly of your fellow man—the very same folly that used to overwhelm and depress you. You just need *one additional ingredient* to convert your newfound detachment to controlled folly.

---

[9]   Castaneda, Carlos. *A Separate Reality.* New York: Pocket Books, 1971. Pp. 55-67.

Amusement

That's right: *amusement.* You have to find the Mayhem and folly amusing, perhaps even fascinating. There is no point in being offended, any more than you would be when you see a dog licking his gonads. That's what dogs do. Likewise, humans stir up mayhem and folly. Righteous indignation is useless. You'll never stop their mayhem or the folly, so why fume about it?

This feeling of amusement about the folly of mankind is your ticket back into the game of life. You are no longer depressed or anxious about the craziness around you or the pressure others place on you. You are amused by it.

You wade into whatever situations you encounter with a sense of freedom and abandon. *You say and do whatever you want, not what you assume others expect of you.* You might even accept a few monkeys now and then, just for the fun of it. You might throw off your heels and zoom around the party after young Travis and Tammy, letting yourself feel as unhinged as they are.

Not Funny

Sounds easy enough, but you might rightfully ask, how can one be amused by the most despicable aspects of the Mayhem, such as serial killers, child molesters, genocide, human trafficking, starvation and malnutrition, climate change, and mass extinction, to name a few. You cannot, of course. Even someone as glib as I am cannot ask you to do that.

Thanks to the digital evolution of mass media, all the daunting tribulations around the world are thrust into our consciousness with unrelenting regularity. It's enough to make us lose our smiles permanently.

However, rarely do these disasters strike our daily life. We "experience" them in a disembodied way as we read about them or watch news feeds. This chaos is not assaulting us directly, and in many cases, there is little to nothing we can do about it. But we still feel shitty and helpless about being forced to witness the Mayhem vicariously.

Hack Five: U Do U gives you the means to combat the existential malaise caused by the Mayhem served up by the media. You ask and answer The Question, "Who do I want to be in relation to this?" If you want to join the fray and work diligently to stop human trafficking, for example, then you throw yourself wholeheartedly into the movement, controlling your folly as you cope with all the idiotic, man-made obstacles you are sure to encounter.

Such an unconstrained commitment can be a valuable and rewarding use of your life force. Helping others in need reduces depression and anxiety through a powerful diversion from your own shit show and a priceless feeling of human bonding.

If, on the other hand, you decide not to participate in a given cause, you say "not my circus" and you stop thinking about it. *Give it no more energy.* Maybe you cannot find anything amusing about human trafficking, but the preservation of your life force demands you do not fret about it unless and until you intend to do something about it.

In essence, any news or reality outside your immediate sphere of influence that depresses you or increases your anxiety must be bitch-slapped away. You must be free of this emotional baggage so you can enthusiastically return to controlling your folly in your daily life. I realize this sounds harsh and uncaring, but—if you contemplate this issue—you might agree it's the only sensible response.

Does this mean you have to stop binging on news feeds about inhumanity towards animals, nature and our fellow man? Perhaps it does. If daily news feeds diminish your life force, you will be better off without them.

Empathy or Admiration

Are you still unwilling or unable to find amusement in the Mayhem and folly of the human condition? That's not surprising. Amusement implies a feeling of lightheartedness that's antithetical to depression and anxiety. Occasional flares of amusement might arise more easily and more often when your emotional set point tracks closer to Neutral. For now, you might have to settle for *empathy* as your path to connect with those around you.

Surely you can picture the shit show running in the heads of many people you know. They are getting micro-cut all day long by The Beast, just as you are. They're fretting about what others think of their words and actions. They're defending their damaged egos and lugging around their ponderous self-importance, while doing their best to wander through the folly and Mayhem of their personal foam pits. How about a little empathy?

Perhaps you know a few impressive souls who manage their folly in a manner you envy. They seem balanced, successful, satisfied, and happy-go-lucky. Maybe they are. Your envy is well justified, but it does not serve you. It drains your life force. Instead, tell your Beast to shut the hell up and try to generate a bit of *admiration*. Hey, these (few) folks really are controlling their folly. They found a way to enjoy the foam pit. They are more than amused—they are engaged! Hats off to them!

My point is simple (like pretty much everything else I've been saying). When the tools of *Hack Five: U Do U* unhook you from the folly and Mayhem, *you can maintain a genuine feeling of connection with the rest of humanity by generating a touch of amusement, empathy, or admiration.* Then get right back to bitch-slapping, smacking-back, and controlling your folly.

Useless Judgment

Maybe more than a few readers are annoyed with me for recommending amusement, empathy, and admiration as a pathway to human connection. You may insist, "Why should I give a shit about people? They're all self-centered clowns!" While I don't admire that point of view, I can empathize, and I do find it amusing.

Ask yourself, "Does being judgmental benefit me or my life force?" Of course not! Imagine for a moment how much more pleasant your day will be without a continual stream of negative, judgmental thoughts about people, including yourself. You'll be better off without them.

Your torrent of judgmental thoughts does not even belong to you; you are merely observing it as it sails through. Why invest your life force in it? Why not assume these judgments are generated by The Beast, just like all your other shitty thoughts? Get rid of them by bitch-slapping them away. This works well in most situations.

For example, you are at a business cocktail party and are introduced to an expert in your field who possibly could be helpful to your career. Immediately upon shaking his hand, your Beast goes to work. "Jeez, look at the gnarly tufts of hair sticking out of his ears and nose! How gross! And his teeth are so yellow! And his breath smells like rancid cigar smoke, ugh!" You frown. You start to pull away. Your body language grows anxious, and he immediately senses it.

In this case, your most sensible response is to bitch-slap the hell out of The Beast and get on with the conversation. We're not asking you to cohabitate with the guy, for chrissake!

Releasing shitty judgments gets more challenging when you are stuck with the offensive person for extended periods of time. Let's say your mother-in-law has a grating, nervous laugh reminiscent of fingernails being dragged across a chalkboard. She's visiting for four days over Thanksgiving, and, thirty minutes into the holiday, your nerves are already torched from her constant, shrill cackling. Bitch-slapping is not working, and amusement, empathy, and admiration are out of the question. What can you do to preserve your life force and survive the holiday weekend?

Reflexive Forgiveness

It took me more than one hundred pages to broach the idea of forgiveness, but it's your best option in situations like this. I do not mean the profound, hard-earned forgiveness you achieve after years of psychotherapy or meditation. I am talking about *reflexive forgiveness* that's only a short step from bitch-slapping.

This automatic forgiveness is sensible because we all are damaged goods in one form or another. In contrast to the famous maxim of the best-selling self-help book of 1967, *I'm OK—You're OK*, reflexive forgiveness relies on the assumption, "I'm a little screwy—you're a little screwy." The annoying traits and behaviors of others are the essence of *Mayhem with the Misfits*, and they are inevitable and unavoidable. The sun will rise tomorrow, bills will arrive, and people will do dumb shit, including each of us. It is far easier to forgive Mayhem and folly as it arises than to live in persistent negative judgment of it.

Which seems better for your life force, reflexive judgment or reflexive forgiveness?

Implementing reflexive forgiveness is easy for skilled bitch-slappers like you. As each negative judgment arises, instead of saying "Shut the hell up," you simply say, "I forgive that, I forgive that, I forgive that." Each time your mother-in-law cackles, you simply think, "I forgive that." You'll agree it's much more pleasant than grinding your teeth, and, in time, you might even find her amusing.

Becoming Unfuckwithable

Hack Five: U Do U is the coup de grâce in our efforts to transform you from being fucked up and fucked over to being **unfuckwithable**. This term has been around for a while, but I picked it up from Vishen Lakhiani, the founder of Mind Valley and author of *The Code of the Extraordinary Mind*. I like the word a lot because when you can honestly agree that it applies to you, my work here is nearly done. Our efforts to transform you from Dominat*ed* to Dominat*or* have succeeded when you feel unfuckwithable.

You now possess simple but powerful hacks to deal *in the moment* with most of the threats to your life force that pound you continually. You first beat back your internal Beast through bitch-slapping, diversion, and appreciation. Now you can cope with external Shit-Slingers and the Mayhem of the Misfits, thanks to The Question, the Dodge/Smack-back/High Road Smack-back/ Broken Record responses, and your amused participation in the folly of your fellow humans.

Your single-minded vigilance to protect your life force has shifted your priority away from worrying what others think about you. You are finally free to decide in each situation who and how you want to be. You are most of the way to being unfuckwithable, are you not? And we still have two more hacks!

Nobody's Victim

I have to mention one crucial corollary to your achievement of unfuckwithablility. Once you embrace being unfuckwithable, you dispense with an entire category of shitty thoughts: those related to victimhood. Until recently, you have been somebody's victim, have you not? Perhaps it's a Shit Slinger or two, or a Misfit, or the gods, or fate, or your sordid past, or the human condition, or whatever story The Beast dreams up to torture you. Hopefully, you are viciously bitch-slapping all thoughts related to victimhood, as they all undoubtedly feel shitty. *You are nobody's victim.* Get used to it. Take a moment to look at yourself in the mirror, stare intently into your own eyes, and declare, "Whose victim am I? *NOBODY'S!*"

Now, close this book and devote the next week or two to studying your external world. Observe the people and forces that diminish your life force *as it happens*. Then immediately and diligently apply the hacks you learned in these two chapters.

When you feel unfuckwithable for at least a couple days in a row, join me back here for *Hack Six*, which helps you hack the day-to-day issues sapping your life force.

Hack Six: The Daily Grind

OK, all you unfuckwithable, bitch-slapping, back-smacking, monkey-flinging, folly controllers, let's see if we can upgrade your daily grind to the point of tolerable. We've dealt directly and effectively with the shit show in your head and the Shit Slingers in your life. Now let's hack your daily grind—the draining activities of your daily life—to further juice your flow of life force. Ready?

Because you animate a physical body—basically lugging it around with you—most of your life is spent on *maintenance*. Your body needs food, sleep, a domicile, clothing, grooming, exercise, transportation, health care, and enough money to provide all this stuff for you, your family, and your pets.

Oddly, you're obliged to compete against others to get that money, too. The basic maxim of life on Earth, *eat or be eaten*, still applies metaphorically to us in our capitalist society. You claw your way high enough up whatever pyramid you occupy in order to maintain your lifestyle. Whenever possible, you acquire and stockpile far more assets than you need, to safeguard against every conceivable crisis that could knock you and yours off the pyramid.

Take a few moments now to recall your activities over the last 48 hours. Ask yourself why you did each thing. How much of it was dedicated to *maintenance* in one form or another, either for yourself or your dependents? How many of your activities did you feel obligated to do, versus those you simply wanted to do?

If you are depressed or anxious, it's a safe bet the scale tips heavily towards obligation. Chronic feelings of obligation exhaust life force. When you reduce your maintenance obligations, you bolster your life force. How can we do this? Our first step is to examine your *wants* versus your *needs*.

Want Versus Need

Desire is a core aspect of being human. Our consciousness erupts with a continual stream of desires. If you doubt that, just sit motionless for a couple of minutes, and I guarantee you will want something, be it food, drink, a trip to the bathroom, to check your smartphone, to talk to someone, to go back to bed, to shop online, to "pleasure" yourself, whatever. Perhaps desire is merely a tool The Beast uses to torture us, but I believe it runs deeper than that.

Beyond the basic drive to survive, most of us have an ingrained desire to improve, to be more, to do more, to have more. The continual frustration of this desire fuels depression and anxiety. In our society, this desire has been manipulated and warped beyond redemption, putting most of us on the treadmill of competition and materialistic acquisition that ultimately fails to satisfy.

If you've been fortunate enough to acquire all the material crap you craved—designer clothes, luxury autos, McMansions, vacation homes, jewelry, art—you've probably already learned that nice things rarely deliver lasting happiness. Instead, you quickly get accustomed to them, take them for granted, and hunger for more. They also create more maintenance headaches.

Likewise, embracing the rat race—getting straight A's in school, attending an Ivy League university, getting hired at a top investment fund or law firm—often leads to ennui and disillusionment after years, or even decades, of grinding it out day after day. Chasing success or money in a career you don't enjoy is a treadmill to despair.

At the other end of the spectrum, lots of folks really just want to party and screw off, so they wander through each day in a disjointed fog until at some point they wake up long enough to realize their life prospects utterly suck. As The Beast pounds them with regrets, they realize crass hedonism is no more fulfilling than the rat race.

Obviously, I don't know your exact situation, but you probably have plenty of things you once wanted and now don't need. You're spending too much time on obligations and maintenance and not enough time on activities you truly enjoy. That's why you don't give a shit about tomorrow's sunrise. Is this true for you?

Fortunately, we won't process your unfulfilled desires, broken dreams, wasted money, and lost years. We'll simply pare down the unnecessary maintenance shit in your daily grind, so you can fill your bucket of emotional energy by doing more things you enjoy—at least a little bit. Let's get hacking.

The Thumb Test

Hack Six: The Daily Grind is absurdly easy to remember and relatively easy to implement. **You embrace activities that increase your life force and discard activities that diminish your life force.** While simple in concept, *Hack Six* can bring earthshaking consequences. Odds are, you'll make significant changes to your daily grind. The techniques are simple, starting with the Thumb Test.

To give you a framework you can deploy in real time, let's modify Eckhart Tolle's concept of Awakened Doing. In Tolle's words, "If you are not in the state of either *acceptance, enjoyment, or enthusiasm*, look closely and you will find that you are creating suffering for yourself and others."[10] Ideally, you are *enthusiastic* about whatever you are doing at the present moment. If not, maybe you can still *enjoy* it. No? Well, at a minimum, you *accept* it. Anything less depletes your life force.

Hack Six: The Daily Grind asks you to apply a similar— but simpler—filter to your daily activities, especially those you repeat over and over, day after day. As you approach an activity, ask yourself how spending time on it will affect your life force. Thumbs-up, thumbs-down, or neutral?

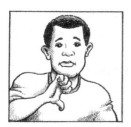

Apply the Thumb Test to any particularly annoying task you do every week. Pick the worst one—a definite thumbs-downer. Can you *stop* doing it? If not, can you *barter* or *outsource* to get someone else to do it? If not, can you *reframe* it into something more tolerable? Worst case, you might need the *nuclear option*.

---

[10] Tolle, Eckhart. *A New Earth: Awakening to Your Life's Purpose*. UK: Penguin Books, 2016. Pp. 295.

Let's start with an easy example. Suppose you spend nearly an hour grooming every morning to start your day. How do you feel *today* about doing this? What's your immediate reaction? Thumbs-up or neutral? Go for it! Thumbs-down? Do something different.

Maybe you say, "I really like the way I feel when I am groomed, so it's worth the time." No problem, go for greatness. On the other hand, perhaps you get the thumbs-down, but The Beast declares you look like hell without shaving/makeup. First, you bitch slap The Beast. You then say, "Screw it, I don't care if I look like a zombie; I'm going grubby today." Thumbs-up! You truncate your grooming routine and head out into the day with a little jolt of extra life force.

Occasionally, the thumb test requires a little extra thought, though. For example, it is time to get ready for your daily workout. You're tired and start to give it a thumbs-down. You think again and recall you typically feel better after the workout and you'll reap the benefits of increased energy, fitting into your clothes, fewer health issues, etc. So, your thumb moves up to neutral and you get on with the workout. The simple act of issuing a thumb-rating before continuing preserves your life force.

Barter and Outsource

When you can't dump a thumbs-down maintenance issue entirely, look for a way to barter or outsource it to someone else, such as a family member, friend, co-worker, neighbor, or someone you hire on the Internet.

For example, imagine you've been making breakfast or dinner for your spouse and kids for years. They take your efforts for granted, no one offers to help, and this maintenance task is getting a big thumbs-down. Regardless of what The Beast or any of these Shit Slingers have to say, you have to make a change.

You might announce that, from now on, the family members will rotate daily responsibility for making and serving the meal. You'll be available to train and assist them for the next thirty days, after which they'll be on their own. If they don't participate, they don't eat. Sure, holy hell is liable to break loose, but your life force is bound to spike upward.

If you are sick of housework, laundry, cooking, dog-walking, yard work, organizing, shopping, whatever, find someone else to do it. Barter by offering to do something you like that they don't. Hire neighborhood kids for cheap. Sure, their results won't be as polished as when you do it, but who cares, really? Assuming you live long enough, *you will ultimately outsource all your maintenance issues*, including wiping your own butt, so you might as well start now.

Think for a minute and decide how you can barter or outsource at least one thumbs-down maintenance issue in your daily grind, and write what you will do with the time you free up.

Task _____

Barter/Outsource _____

Free Time _____

Reframing

At times, your life situations are complicated or nuanced, and quitting, outsourcing, and bartering are lousy options. Imagine you have accepted a new job you really like, but the ninety-minute commute each way in heavy traffic is more daunting than you expected. You can't move closer to work because you're locked into a long-term lease, your wife works an hour away in the opposite direction, or your kids go to great schools. It's a rainy Monday morning, and your upcoming commute is a colossal thumbs-down. The Beast calls you moronic for accepting a job so far away. You need to *reframe* the situation.

Reframing means *assigning a different purpose or value to the activity*, finding a way to make it neutral or better on the thumb meter. In the case of your shitty commute, you layer additional activities into the time. Get a car with dynamic cruise control and a great sound system. Use the time to learn a new language, listen to audio books or podcasts, or ride share with interesting people who will debate current affairs or social media gossip. Plaster your car with advertising to earn extra money as you drive. Keep trying different ideas until you hit on something that reframes the activity and maintains or improves your life force. The ride might even transform into a thumbs-up endeavor.

Sometimes reframing requires a big shift. I recall a story my mom recounted about living with her two toddler sons in an isolated apartment, without a car, while my Dad traveled a lot for business. She was going bat-shit crazy. One day, Dad returned from a trip to learn the family was moving! Mom had found an affordable townhouse in a new neighborhood teeming with other kids and their young mothers. She had reframed stay-at-home motherhood into something more tolerable and life force enhancing.

No doubt you have at least one daunting, thumbs-down situation that requires some serious reframing. You don't have to solve it all at once! But you do have to put yourself on a path to a better condition. Just knowing you are on that path will bolster your life force and grant you patience. Take a few minutes to test your reframing abilities on one of your enduring maintenance challenges.

Issue _____

Reframe_____

The Nuclear Option

The Nuclear Option was inaccessible prior to *Hack Six*, because it requires a reservoir of life force you lacked until now. You had to cope effectively with The Beast, the Shit Slingers, the Mayhem and the folly before you could even consider blowing up your daily grind.

Having mastered the first five hacks, you now can silence The Beast and Shit Slingers long enough to really examine your daily grind. Can you accept your current life circumstances and still achieve an emotional set point close to Neutral? Can you control your folly and sustain your life force by dumping, outsourcing, and reframing most of the thumbs-down items in your daily grind? Are there really that many?

Hopefully, the mental show in your head has become less of a shit show, and you realize your current situation is good enough for now. I believe this will be the case for most of us because The Beast and Shit Slingers spawn most of our depression and anxiety. Once those nefarious forces are controlled, the remaining nuances of the daily grind usually comprise small potatoes.

Nevertheless, we must discuss scenarios that call forth the Nuclear Option. The silencing of The Beast and the steady increase in your life force finally lifts the heavy veil of your depression and anxiety enough for you to see that, hey, your daily grind really is intolerable and you finally possess enough energy to push the red button and blow it the hell up.

Obvious examples of the Nuclear Option include walking out on your spouse and kids; telling your abysmal boss to shove this pathetic job up his or her puckered old arse; dropping out, selling all your stuff, hitting the road in an RV; and quitting school and hitch-hiking through the snow to the coast, etc. The life force is flowing again, baby, and it's time for a little scorched earth!

Can the Nuclear Option work? Can going nuclear lead to a radical, sustainable upsurge in life force? I believe it can— *sometimes*. I once knew a psychotherapist who extracted herself from a toxic marriage and later found a terrific guy; they lived happily ever after in his $18 million home in Woodside, California. We've all heard stories of Wall Street hedge fund managers who threw it all in to operate a boutique resort in Barbados or raise llamas in the Himalayas. Good shit can happen, post-apocalypse.

However, recall my postulation that the dominant theme of humanity is Mayhem with the Misfits. You want to be careful you aren't jumping out of the proverbial frying pan into the proverbial fire. To go nuclear, you can't be spontaneous, impetuous, or cavalier; you need to be strategic, organized, and patient. Let's consider a few examples.

Say you are trapped in an abusive relationship. You've used our first five hacks to clear your mind enough to realize and fully admit your mate is a Shit Slinger of the worst kind. You're dependent on him financially and you have two young kids. Your gut is now screaming that you have to cut him out of your daily grind, and you're ready to grab the kids and run.

Or imagine you're starting to loathe your successful career as a social media influencer. You've been pulling in twenty-five to fifty grand a month in sponsorship fees as your followers multiply on YouTube, Facebook, Instagram, Twitter, TikTok, and Snap. However, you wake up every morning to a panic attack when you think of the grind of daily posts on all channels, the pressure of having your life on public display, and the thousands of shitty hate comments you get every day. With your leased Ferrari and posh penthouse on Wilshire Boulevard—not to mention your entourage of mooching "friends"—you're spending every penny you earn, and maybe a bit more. Your daily grind is eating you alive and you're about to shut it all down, stop posting, and let the shit hit the fan.

Or maybe you're an outstanding, straight-A student, athlete, and musician starting your senior year of high school. Your daily treadmill runs relentlessly from pre-dawn until after midnight. You're concealing your growing anxiety and depression as you prepare your fourteen applications to top-tier universities, but the sad fact is you hate your life, dread the future, and want to run away from home and get stoned into oblivion.

Of course, none of the responses proposed above appear likely to improve these unhappy situations, do they? Impetuously blowing up the status quo causes more trauma ahead. The trick to winning with the Nuclear Option is to develop and implement a plan. Sure, your current situation might end with a big bang, but only after your escape path has been carefully laid out.

At this point in the book, you've beaten back The Beast, smacked-back the Shit Slingers to a stand-still, dodged monkeys and controlled your folly, and entertained the idea of dumping, outsourcing, and reframing the unsavory elements of your daily grind. Your life force is on the rise. If your improved mental clarity insists your daily grind has to be blown up, you must devote your increased life force to planning and executing your transformation.

In the famous words of Stephen Covey, "Begin with the end in mind."[11] Decide what you want your situation to be in, say, two or three years. Paint your ideal picture in as much detail as possible. Sketch out your first thoughts on everything that has to happen between now and then. List your resources and possible allies. Write down annual and monthly goals and ideas for achieving them. Be strategic, be clever, be sly, be precise. The process should take you *at least* a few hours. Even if it takes a month, it's worth it.

A word of caution: If you lack the energy and commitment to work through a strategy and plan, you have no hope of succeeding with the Nuclear Option. Hold off for now!

One of two things will happen when you actually go through the head banging of creating your nuclear strategic plan. Either you will decide implementing the plan requires way too much effort and you should focus instead on some incremental changes in your current daily grind, or you will say, "Yes, damn it, I can and will do this." Either way, your life force will be sustained.

I generally don't advocate resorting to the Nuclear Option, for a couple of reasons. First, the planetary theme of Mayhem with the Misfits conspires with the Law of Unintended Consequences

---

[11] Covey, Stephen R. *The 7 Habits of Highly Effective People*. Provo, UT: Franklin Covey, 1998. P. 52

to make glorious dreams achingly hard to achieve. This observation flies in the face of upbeat instruction from famous athletes and entertainers who tell you to dream big and pursue your dreams at all costs. Such advice worked great for those standouts, obviously, but not so well for the countless others who risked everything and ended up broke and disillusioned in middle age. Take such guidance with a grain of salt.

Second, as I postulated aggressively at the beginning of this book, the primary source of your depression and anxiety is the shit show in your head. Fix that, and most of the unpleasant machinations of your daily grind fade in importance.

Returning to our three scenarios above, two probably call for merely modifying the daily grinds. Our social media influencer could spend less money, post less often, do more collabs, kick out the freeloaders, and block the stream of hate comments, while s/he investigates working behind the camera in the future.

Our over-achieving student could get a few B's, drop a few sports or music commitments, apply to fewer colleges, and free up some time for fun. Both of these individuals must continue to bitch-slap The Beast and smack-back with their Shit Slingers, who surely will condemn these changes to their daily grinds.

Only the abused mother of two needs to nuke her current situation, and she must do so with utmost cunning and caution. Running out the door with no forethought would prove fruitless at best. With help from external resources, such as the National Domestic Abuse Hotline or local services, she could develop and implement an escape plan that consumes weeks or months, yet provides a safe landing for her and the kids. In the interim, her life force would be sustained by the confidence that a viable path to secure freedom is opening to her and her children.

Most likely, you will resort to the Nuclear Option only once or twice in your long life. The rest of the time you can hack your daily grind by dumping, outsourcing, or reframing those maintenance tasks that tax your life force. Each small improvement gives you more energy to "be the boss of you" and demonstrate who you really want to be in this foam pit of our multi-dimensional universe.

Fun Time

Hacking your daily grind frees time for activities you might enjoy. The final step of *Hack Six* is to carve out a little fun time every day.

Recall the Fifteen Second Routine from *Hack Four: Feeling Good-ish*. Wake up in the morning and run the three-finger TBI routine: say thanks, bless someone, and now I want you to devote your five-second *intent* to doing something fun that day. Start with at least one activity every day that brings you some enjoyment. Make a list below of activities you intend to do more often.

_____ _____ _____

_____ _____ _____

_____ _____ _____

Over time, increase enjoyable activities until they comprise a hefty part of your day. At that point, you'll have successfully hacked your daily grind.

Can I assume you're developing confidence and skill with the first five hacks? If so, *Hack Six: The Daily Grind* will slip easily into your bag of tricks for increasing your life force and moving your emotional set point consistently closer to Neutral. Give yourself a day or two to hack your daily grind, then return for our final hack. *Hack Seven: Chief Body Officer* promises to upgrade your relationship with your body and further boost your life force.

Hack Seven: Chief Body Officer

Like it or not, you are the chairperson of a massive organization. Yes, you are the Big Boss of about *seventy trillion* living cells toiling away in your body right now. That number is nearly *ten thousand times* the number of people on Earth! As a paltry point of reference, Walmart, currently the world's largest private employer, supervises only about 2.3 million employees. Hell, your organization replaces about three hundred million dead cells *every second*. You and your body are absolutely amazing!

How are you doing as the Big Boss? Does your executive performance suck? Should you be fired? Don't worry; you are irreplaceable, with guaranteed lifetime employment. If you abandon your post, the whole organization shuts down— permanently.

In *Hack Seven*, we transform your body into a cherished ally, instead of a burden or a foe. Hopefully, you'll learn to love your perpetual title of Chief Body Officer (CBO).

Bodily Functions

Every societal organization exists for a stated purpose. Likewise, our bodies serve specific functions. First, they're in the *housing and transportation* business, housing our consciousness and transporting it around the physical foam pit of our multidimensional universe, so we can participate fully in the Mayhem and folly.

Next, our bodies are in the *service* business. They serve the machinations of our monkey minds as we pursue grand dreams and feckless schemes. We get up every morning and tell our bodies what to do, and trillions of minions strive to comply.

Human bodies are in the *storage* business, too. Our bodies absorb and carry energetic echoes of powerful emotions we've had in the past. These deep feelings color and affect most aspects of our present awareness. This is our "emotional baggage," and some of us spend small fortunes with therapists trying to unload it.

Most incredibly, our bodies are in the *health care* business. Our devoted teams of cells and organs strive to keep all systems running smoothly, no matter what we throw at them. Take your best shot: Poison your body with alcohol and drugs, dehydrate it, starve it, overfeed it crappy food, run it to exhaustion, crash it into stuff, expose it to deadly germs and toxins, deny it rest and exercise, and yet your miraculous body tries to heal itself and keep on keepin' on—for a good while, anyway.

To please us, our bodies learn to anticipate, even crave, whatever we give it repeatedly. Be it healthy food, fattening food, long bike rides, TV binge-watching, afternoon naps, drugs, or booze, our bodies acclimate to whatever we throw at them, and, in time, they beg for more. If your body is nagging you ceaselessly for something, at some point it came first from you.

The Beast and Your Body

In light of your body's miraculous capabilities and unswerving loyalty to you, we might expect you to be highly appreciative and affectionate toward it. Probably, though, you are not.

Are there things you don't like about your body? It is too fat, too skinny, too tall, too short, too dark, too light, too old, too something or not enough of something else? Maybe you dislike your bulbous nose, your three chins, your sallow complexion, your buggy eyes, your baggy skin, your love handles, your skinny legs, or your saggy ass. Do you compare your body to someone else's or to your imaginary ideal, and find it lacking? You probably wish you had a different, better body, right?

If so, don't even worry about it! Recall that your Beast is using the so-called shortcomings of your body to slash you with micro-cuts and devour your life force. Let's deploy *Hack Seven: Chief Body Officer* to reframe your relationship with your body and increase your life force.

Running Your Organization

As the chief executive of your bodacious organization, you have two main jobs, similar to those of any CEO of a Fortune 500 company. First, you devise the vision, goals, and strategy of your empire. Then, you procure the resources your team needs to achieve its lofty goals.

Huh? What does this have to do with your body? OK, maybe anointing you the chief executive of your body seems like a stupid idea. Still, you have entertained my other ludicrous ideas—hopefully with some benefit—so stick with me for a few more pages, OK? Our goal is to reframe your thinking about your body in a manner that feels better on a moment-by-moment basis, day after day. It works for me!

Vision, Goals, & Strategy

Your seventy trillion cells comprise your most valuable asset. Would you sell your eyeballs for a million dollars? Maybe an arm or a leg? How about your tongue? Not likely, right?

How do you view this valuable organization you own and operate? You maintain a mental conception of your current body, and it's probably not pleasant. Starting immediately, discard that idea and generate a new mental image of your ideal body. Substitute that new image every time your Beast slams you with a shitty thought about your body. Bitch-slap The Beast and insert the new-body vision, over and over and over.

For example, let's assume you are a male in your mid-forties, balding, double-chinned, paunchy, about forty pounds overweight, with a tricky back and a bum knee. Whenever you think of your body, you think "ugh," and your life force takes a little hit. The Beast does not even have to say anything; you get the shitty feeling the instant you imagine your body.

Now, instead, I want you to take a few seconds to imagine your body looks and feels like Arnold Schwarzenegger's body when he was crowned Mr. Universe in 1968. (If you don't like Arnold, pick some other buff guy or gal.) How does that feel? A little better, right?

My point here is simple: It feels surprisingly good to imagine your body as better looking, healthier, fitter than it is right now. Every time you think of your body, forget your current, "realistic" image, and insert your ideal vision for your body. *As CBO of your body, this is your vision responsibility in action.*

Am I being ridiculous here? No, I am being unrealistic, which is different than being ridiculous. Imagining your body as it really is continually diminishes your life force. Stop being so realistic! Picture your body in whatever manner pleases you. Do it now. Enjoy the exercise. You'll probably elicit a chuckle.

You might expect me to tell you this envisioning exercise is awesomely powerful because you will marshal incredible creative forces on the etheric and astral planes, which will inevitably manifest your better body on the physical plane when propelled by sufficient belief, imagination, and emotion. But I won't because I have no clue if that's true. (In fact, I wonder if optimistic promises about positive thinking are a source of unfulfilled expectations and broken dreams.) I only claim you'll experience a small, pleasant jolt of life force every time you pretend you inhabit your ideal body.

As Chief Body Officer, you shouldn't allow your organization to do whatever the hell it wants with no direction from you. You need to give your body some direction, some *goals*.

When setting your CBO goals, bear in mind that your organization has strong homeostatic tendencies. It assiduously manages many variables, such as core body temperature, blood sugar, levels of iron, calcium, sodium, potassium, and a host of others, within tight ranges.

Your body doesn't appreciate large or unexpected changes in its internal dynamics or its external circumstances. If you've been drinking a fifth of bourbon every day, and you suddenly switch to a quart of goat's milk (or vice versa), your body will freak out—at least until it gets accustomed to the change.

Therefore, most of us should set evolutionary, not revolutionary, goals for our bodies. For example, don't start on a crash diet to lose fifty pounds, cut your calories in half for a week, fall off the wagon on Sunday night and give up a week later. You'll be disappointed with yourself, hate your fat body, and give The Beast more ammo to rain down on you.

Instead, don't even set a goal to lose weight. Set an easy goal, one you might actually implement long term. Dream up a so-called "process goal," such as drinking a big glass of water before every meal so your stomach will feel full and you'll eat less. Every time you achieve a little process goal for your body, you'll get a little jolt of life force—and that's what we're looking for.

Take a moment to dream up and write down one or two simple process goals that will benefit your organization.

_____

_____

_____

_____

_____

_____

Even modest process goals require a little *strategy* to help you achieve them. Your strategy might simply be a new behavior that reminds you to make the change you want, a way to break your homeostatic behavioral routines. For instance, you could fill three large glasses of water in the morning, to increase the likelihood of you seeing and drinking one glass before each meal.

Is my namby-pamby vision, goals, and strategy advice sounding ridiculously simplistic and far too easy for you? If so, that's good! It suggests your life force is creeping up, and your emotional set point is getting closer to Neutral. You're no longer so wickedly depressed you can't drum up the energy to imagine yourself inhabiting Mr. Universe's body or drinking a big glass of water before dinner. If you want to generate more ambitious goals for your body, I'm happy about that. (Can you believe we're even talking about "ambitious goals"?)

Resources

The most important aspect of being CBO is providing the resources your organization needs to prosper. As we noted in *Hack Six*, you devote most of your daily grind to maintenance issues, many of which relate to your body, right? You provide food, shelter, clothing, and a shit-ton of other stuff to keep your umpteen trillion cells operating at full efficiency. You know what your body needs to thrive. Are you delivering the goods?

Provisioning resources gets really tricky if you've trained your body to crave goods and experiences that actually harm it in the long run. For example, if you blitz your body with high doses of pot, booze, nicotine, OxyContin, jelly donuts, or just about anything else before long it nags the hell out of you for more and more. You spend all your time trying to satisfy your body's insistent demands, even while realizing you're only hurting yourself. Does your body do this to you?

As CBO, you have to make tough decisions about your response to each of the incessant pleas from your body. Tell me, are you going to cave in to its nagging for whatever vices you trained it to crave, or will you give it mostly what you know it needs to thrive?

You might ask, "So, Michael, what's my resource allocation hack? What's the simple solution to overriding my body's demands and doing the right thing, time after time?" Sadly, I have no clever or pithy resolution to this conundrum, but I can offer a couple of useful concepts to consider.

The first requirement is *accepting your CBO responsibility*. You are the Big Boss of your body. From this moment on, you never forget who runs the organization. Just as you have bitch-slapped the unrelenting Beast into occasional abeyance, you must apply the same mindset to bringing your demanding body under your command. You might try the Broken Record technique on your body. Just say, "in a minute, in a minute" a few million times a day!

Next, realize that *your massive, homeostatic organization needs to evolve slowly in the direction you want*. Be endlessly patient yet persistent with your goals and strategies. Forget failures and backsliding and focus only on the present moment.

For example, let's say you got carried away last night by mixing assorted pills and alcohol and smoking cheap cigars, and you spent the wee hours yodeling into the porcelain throne. This morning, your head is pounding, your body feels like shit, and The Beast is feeding ferociously on your life force. Are you going to spend the day feeling like a pitiful failure? No! Shake it off! Focus on what resources you need to give your organization right now to make today a better day. (Maybe a double dose of Pedialyte?)

In the beginning, you might lose more often than you win, but over time your organization will conform to your demands. To paraphrase the immortal words of Calvin Coolidge, Ray Kroc and a host of others, "Persistence alone is omnipotent." Be omnipotent!

The Real Value of a Stronger Body

By now, we all agree the essential purpose of this book is to jack up the life force flowing through you in each moment. Your body is a major part of the life force equation. Devoting resources to improving your body chemistry boosts your life force and even reduces the amount of bitch-slapping you have to do.

How so? Your body chemistry influences your thoughts and emotions, which we have identified as key determinants of your life force and emotional set point. Shitty chemistry yields shitty thoughts and shitty emotions.

If you're skeptical that body chemistry can strongly influence your *thoughts*, try dropping a tab of LSD, drinking a pint of whiskey, or staying awake for forty-eight hours straight—or, perish the thought, try all three at once! I guarantee you'll agree with me.

To verify the effect of body chemistry on your *emotions*, consider your nasty morning mood when the alarm goes off after a late night devoted to abusing food and drink, or recall how ragged and razor-sharp your temper becomes after a long, stressful week of working, studying, or parenting. On a more positive note, plenty of research shows that physical exercise stimulates the production of endorphins, which reduce feelings of depression. Clearly, your thoughts and emotions respond to changes in your body chemistry, *which you influence by your resource allocations.*

Wait, am I contradicting myself? Did I not insist shitty thoughts are served up by The Beast, the foreign installation intent on devouring your life force? Well, actually I said we have no idea where our thoughts come from, and The Beast is as good an explanation as any. Let me zig-zag my way around this apparent contradiction by recalling the fable of *The Three Little Pigs*.

The three pigs are siblings who each build a house of different materials. The first two do piss-poor jobs with lousy materials, while the third knocks herself out building a bodacious brick house. The Big Bad Wolf (a.k.a The Beast) shows up and easily blows down the first two pigs' houses, made of straw and sticks respectively. Of course, he devours the first two pigs, life force and all. The third little pig, ensconced securely in her solid brick house, is free to taunt (and bitch-slap) the Big Bad Wolf, who ultimately falls down the brick chimney into the cocky pig's waiting dinner pot.

The moral of this story, as it pertains to your life force, is simply that a strong, healthy, vibrant body is a powerful shield against the endless onslaughts of The Beast. You can guess which of the three little piggies I want you to be!

In other words, I don't believe body chemistry is the sole or even primary source of shitty thoughts and emotions. It is perfectly possible to be in beautiful physical condition and robust health and still be painfully depressed and anxious.

However, I do believe taking good care of your body strengthens your defenses against The Beast. When you are eating, sleeping, and exercising well, your organization runs at peak form and your physical resilience is maximized against The Beast, the Shit Slingers, and the Misfits. A well-run body transmits and channels life force better than a crappy body. Start getting yours today!

Have a Therapeutic Lifestyle Change

While working on this chapter—specifically on resource allocation—I discovered an intriguing, six-step program to beat depression without drugs, developed by Stephan Ilardi Ph.D., a psychotherapist and professor of clinical psychology at University of Kansas. Four of his six steps relate to resources for the body.

Professor Ilardi calls his program Therapeutic Lifestyle Change (TLC), and his clinical research demonstrates that TLC is two to three times more effective for curing depression than medications or cognitive therapy. I shared TLC with a friend who battled depression and anxiety for more than two years. She followed his recommendations and made surprising progress in about three months. I was intrigued!

Here is a quick summary of the six elements of TLC below, distilled from Dr. Ilardi's useful book, *The Depression Cure*.[12]

Brain Food. Omega-3 fats have a proven antidepressant effect, and Professor Ilardi recommends a starting dose of 1000 mg of EPA and 500 mg of DHA to each of his patients, taken in

---

[12] Ilardi, Stephen S. *The Depression Cure: The 6-step Program to Beat Depression without Drugs*. Cambridge, MA: Da Capo Lifelong, 2010.

the form of molecularly distilled (to reduce burping) Omega-3 fatty-acid supplements.

Don't Think, Do. To help you stop endlessly ruminating on your negative thoughts, learn to recognize your negative thought patterns and learn to redirect your focus to another activity. This advice is a light version of our *Hacks One, Two,* and *Three.* As you know, I heartily agree with his "do something else advice" (which I called diversion), yet I believe the relentless shit storm of microcuts also calls for stronger medicine: devoted and energetic bitchslapping.

Antidepressant Exercise. It is well-established that physical exercise changes brain chemistry in a good way and reduces depression better than meds. Give your body at least three 30-minute sessions of aerobic activity per week, with your heart rate up to sixty to seventy-five percent of its maximum for your age. You know this is true, so get moving—once your doctor gives you the green light!

Bright Light Exposure. Depressed people show "perilously low" blood levels of Vitamin D. They need to dramatically increase Vitamin D_3 levels, through daily sun exposure, sessions with a bright light box (depending on their geographic location), and/or by supplementation of Vitamin D_3 per day. Get a blood test to see if you're Vitamin D deficient.

Social Support. Our culture increasingly encourages isolation, yet it is proven that positive social connection with appropriate people reduces depression. Dr. Ilardi offers useful suggestions for increasing your social support structure and making your life more enjoyable. While you are implementing his ideas, be sure to invoke all the hacks you acquired in *Hack Five: U Do U.*

Habits of Healthy Sleep. Loss of slow-wave sleep causes depression, and four of out of five depressed people suffered sleep problems prior to the onset of their condition. TLC offers you ten simple habits to give your body and mind adequate, restorative sleep.

As you can see, four of the six steps in TLC involve resources you should give your body on a consistent basis: Omega-3 fatty acids, aerobic exercise, sunlight and Vitamin D_3 supplementation, and adequate sleep. Dr. Ilardi makes a convincing, compelling case for each of these relatively easy steps.

Whether or not you embrace *The Depression Cure,* I hope you now feel adequate life force to make incremental changes in the resources you give your body every day. Take a minute to declare how you as CBO will provide better resources for your multi-cellular organization. State at least one intention you can stick with!

_____

_____

_____

_____

_____

_____

Excess Storage

Okay, that's enough about providing resources for your body. We have just one more important CBO topic to cover: your *emotional baggage*.

When we're chronically depressed or anxious, our anguish is not entirely due to the ongoing attacks from The Beast and Shit Slingers in our midst and the obligations of the daily grind. Part of the discomfort we feel in each moment is *residual pain* we carry around with us—our emotional baggage. The body clutches at hurts and disappointments and lugs them around from moment to moment, keeping dull, painful emotions close to the surface, so we sense them constantly, long after their initial occurrences.

These feelings are shitty, and they sap your life force, right? To identify this, pause for a moment, focus your attention on the faint, physical sensations in your chest and stomach. Ask yourself, "Do I feel joyous right now?" Most likely, the immediate answer is "No!" If you ask quietly, "What feelings are blocking my joy right now?" you will detect one or more heavy, tight, jumpy, or otherwise unpleasant sensations, each of which is tied to an enduring topic of distress in your life.

These subtle sensations comprise the residual emotional baggage that we must clear out to raise your emotional set point to Neutral and beyond.

Ask yourself to list the theme or cause of each of these shitty, but oh-so-familiar, sensations. Give each a name. Line them up like bowling pins or empty beer bottles. You might be surprised and daunted by how effortlessly the list spills into your consciousness. "Let's see, ooh, there's my first marriage [ouch], there's the second marriage [ugh], there's my kid in prison for selling crystal meth to minors [awk], there's the bloody job I got fired from at the slaughterhouse [shit], there's my overdrawn bank account [crap], there's my drunk driving conviction [damn], there's that unctuous priest who tried to touch me 'down there' in fifth grade," [yuck]... and on and on. Hell, you've got more baggage than the Titanic!

Wouldn't you love to eliminate, or at least reduce, your emotional baggage? Can you agree that any reduction in your heavy load will increase your life force and raise your emotional set point closer to Neutral? How can we do that?

To this point, we've concentrated on protecting your life force from *real-time* assaults. Yes, the point of power is the present moment, thus we have battled the continual stream of shitty thoughts, words, and obligations that diminish your life force. You're well equipped now to bitch-slap, divert, and smack-back incoming attacks the instant they strike.

Perhaps you also noticed that we accomplished this beneficial preservation of your life force without "processing" any of your psychological issues.

We didn't need to!

You might ask, can you also release your stored reservoir of emotional pain without a lot of unpleasant processing? Yes, I believe so, and it's well worth a couple of pages here and maybe some additional effort on your part.

Naturally, I want to give you something easy and relatively painless, in part because I know you still lack the energy to grind, grind, grind on a bunch of unpleasant feelings and topics (which might not help much, anyway). There exist numerous options to try, including newer body-based approaches such as Eye Movement

Desensitization and Reprocessing (EMDR) and Emotional Freedom Techniques (EFT).

The approach I personally found most compelling and useful is called *Focusing*, a technique developed in the 1960s by philosopher and psychologist Eugene Gendlin, who was named the Distinguished Professional Psychologist of the year in 1970 by the American Psychological Association. Gendlin developed a simple, six-step process for achieving conscious awareness of something he called *felt sense* in the body.

Focusing helps users deal with emotionally charged situations in the present moment, yet I also find it beneficial for isolating and releasing long-standing, painful, emotional baggage. It's amazing and perhaps unbelievable that carefully and gently identifying and focusing on the *felt sense* of a troubling issue can trigger a welcome release of toxic emotional energy.

With a little practice, you can easily run through the six steps in a matter of ten to fifteen minutes and experience surprising relief from the long-standing weight of one piece of your emotional baggage. To give you an idea of how simple and straightforward focusing is, I'll paraphrase a summary of the six steps that make up one round of focusing.

If you're skeptical, that's okay; I know it's hard to believe this can work.

Clearing A Space. Direct attention to your body, in your stomach or chest, and ask yourself, "How is my life going? What is the main thing for me right now?" As an issue comes up, acknowledge it and the associated sensation in your body and set it aside. Ask the questions several times until all your main issues are sensed and set aside, like those bowling pins or beer bottles mentioned above.

Felt Sense. Pick just one of the issues. For example, maybe it's "my second marriage and divorce." Stand back from it. Quietly scan your body for an unclear physical sensation that encompasses the entire problem. Take your time. Let yourself feel the unclear sense of all of that emotional weight. This is your *felt sense* of the issue.

Handle. Ask yourself, what is the quality of this unclear felt sense? Be patient. Pretty soon, the felt sense itself will give you a word, a phrase, or an image that sums it up. That's your handle.

Resonating. Spend a few moments going back and forth between the felt sense and the handle, looking for a little bodily signal that says the handle fits well. Let the felt sense and/or the handle change as necessary.

Asking. Now ask yourself, "What is it about this issue that makes this sense so (handle)?" Or ask, "What is in this sense?" Stay with the felt sense till something comes along with a *shift*, a slight "give" or release.

Receiving. Receive whatever comes with the shift, even if it is only a slight release or sense of relief. This is only one shift; there will be others.[13]

My brief description of focusing is unlikely to help you, but it illustrates the simplicity of the process. I recommend you invest a little time on <u>focusing.org</u>, where you'll find everything you need to quickly master this powerful, enjoyable tool for releasing the weight of your emotional baggage.

---

[13] <u>https://focusing.org/sixsteps</u>

Focusing is so simple that I learned to perform a round while walking the dog, driving my car, or waiting in line. If you'll spend ten minutes focusing each day for just one week, I am confident you'll enjoy a delightful feeling of lightheartedness you had long forgotten.

I focus first thing in the morning, right after a little bitch-slapping and my TBI exercise. I run through one or two rounds to release any issues that might be have surfaced during my sleep, so I can start my day with more energy. Give it a try!

You might wonder why I didn't mention focusing at the beginning of this book, so you could dump a bunch of emotional baggage right at the start. Honestly, I thought about it—but I had to assume you lacked the life force needed to work your way through a six step program focused on unpleasant feelings in your body. All I dared to ask for, at that point, was a bit of micro-slash hacking and some persistent bitch-slapping. Now I believe you have enough life force flowing to support a few rounds of focusing!

We invested considerable time into *Hack Seven: Chief Body Officer* because I am convinced the body and mind are symbiotic and co-dependent. Depression and anxiety create a downward spiral for both mind and body, so reversing the spiral requires changes in both mental and physical activity.

At this point in unleashing *The Seven,* you (hopefully) possess the energy and intent needed to embrace your role of Chief Body Officer and to transform your body into a cherished ally. Set your vision, goals, and strategy, and give your body the resources you know it needs, starting today!

You now own all *Seven Life Hacks* needed to be the *Dominator* we envisioned in the opening pages of this little book. I am proud of you! Thank you for hanging in there with me. To finish our discussion, let's consider "What now?"

What Now?

Hey, you did it! You unleashed *The Seven Life Hacks*! Let's see how you're doing. When we started this venture, you were feeling miserable and perhaps contemplating whether to kill yourself.

How are you feeling now? Are you still an enslaved, beaten loser? Or, are you feeling *unfuckwithable*? Or somewhere in between? Have you become a different person, as I predicted on the opening pages of this book? Let's take two minutes for a quick review of *The Seven* and evaluate where you stand. See how many of these questions you can honestly answer in a positive way.

Quick Review

Hack One: The Micro-Slash. Can you immediately identify each thought that stimulates a shitty feeling in you?

Hack Two: Bitch-Slapping. Did you embrace the metaphor of The Beast who assaults you with shitty thoughts and devours your precious life force? Are you bitch-slapping The Beast with grim determination and/or unbridled enthusiasm?

Hack Three: Diversion. Did you try a few activities to reduce your daily daydreaming, especially during prime micro-slash times? Are your diversions reducing your micro-slashes by fifty percent or more?

Hack Four: Feeling Good-ish. Do you occasionally have the energy and willpower to insert a few thoughts of your own making into the show running in your head? Are you generating a little thankfulness, blessings, or intent of your own invention and doing your Fifteen-Second TBI routine from time to time?

Hack Five: U Do U. Are you asking and answering The Question repeatedly, so you truly can be the boss of you? Are you employing the Dodge, Smack-back, and Broken-Record techniques to deal with Shit Slingers in your midst? Are you using controlled folly, amusement, empathy, and/or admiration to maintain a sense of connection with your fellow humans? Have you felt unfuckwithable?

Hack Six: The Daily Grind. Did you evaluate your daily maintenance issues from the thumbs up/thumbs down perspective? Have you succeeded at bartering, outsourcing, and reframing as many of your thumbs-down activities as possible? Most importantly, are you freeing up a little time each day for fun?

Hack Seven: Chief Body Officer. Have you embraced your role as CBO of your massive organization? Are you giving your body the resources you know it needs versus what you trained it to crave?

If you answered "yes" to even half of these questions, I am proud of you. You must be at least halfway to feeling unfuckwithable, right? If you did not score so well, at least you can quickly sense which hacks you should review and work on more.

We're now ready to check on your emotional set point. Review the exercise you did at the beginning of this book to establish exactly how miserable you were. In the box below, take a shot at estimating your emotional set point range as you mastered each of *The Seven*. Which hack has done you the most good? If you'd like, take a screenshot of your progress and email it to me with your story at The7LifeHacks@gmail.com. I'd love to see it!

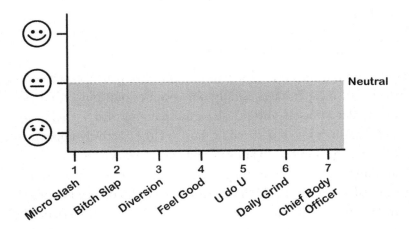

What Now?

"What now" depends on where your life force and emotional set points are presently. If *The Seven* has completely changed your life for the better and you are living with more gusto than a five-year-old at Disneyland, then my work here is done, and you can get on with your life as you see fit.

Perhaps you look back over this book and think, "Jeez, this guy's world view is awfully negative, with his Beast, Mayhem with the Misfits, Shit Slingers, circus monkeys, and daily grind. Why couldn't he present a more upbeat perspective?" If so, your emotional set point is much closer to Neutral, and you are seeing life in a more optimistic vein. I'm glad.

On the other hand, if *The Seven* gave you no relief, you might start by returning the book for a refund! In this case, you are still consumed by thoughts of killing yourself, so let's tackle that issue head-on.

Still Want to Whack Yourself?

For the record, I disagree with the stringent taboo against suicide in most cultures. Oddly, our societies outright forbid you to murder yourself abruptly by gun, hanging, ledge diving, or stepping in front of a speeding bus, yet they actively encourage behaviors guaranteed to kill you slowly, such as excessive smoking, drinking, eating, or pill popping. If you are hell-bent on killing yourself, the speed at which you undertake it should be immaterial. In fact, the quicker methods should be endorsed enthusiastically, because they'd save society a bundle of money in wasted health care expenditures on people indulging their death wishes.

In any event, I do not think folks should be forced to inhabit bodies against their wills, any more than they should be forced to eat their vegetables, watch daytime TV, pierce their noses, marry their second cousins, or dance the polka.

This perspective is especially pertinent for people who suffer from chronic pain or debilitating, terminal illnesses. It's irrational to the point of insanity for a society to insist, "I know you are suffering intolerable pain, but just tough it out until the Lord calls for you, after you've slowly wasted away to nothing." Wait, isn't that cruel and unusual punishment? "Well, in the meantime we can dial up your morphine drip until you are comatose, so you won't suffer." Crazy talk!

The Tricky Part

The tricky part, of course, is *who* exactly goes *where* exactly if you exercise your exit option? We already accepted we have no idea *where our thoughts come from* and no clue *why we are here.* Now we can add a third mystery: *What happens when we die?* I see three general possibilities: 1) your lights go out, permanently; 2) you wake up essentially in the same place, as it was all a dream anyway; 3) you wind up somewhere else or in a different form, which might be better or worse. So, you have about a fifty-fifty chance of getting some relief, assuming the annihilation of your consciousness qualifies as relief.

A popular assertion in metaphysical circles describes a lengthy after-death review of the life just passed, wherein the recently deceased soul (you?) relives, over and over, difficult events until the appropriate lessons are learned, much like Bill Murray's lot in the classic 1993 movie, *Groundhog Day.* Does that sound like a big improvement over your current situation?

In the grand scheme of things, it may be irrelevant whether your consciousness is *here* or *there* because, wherever you go, there *you* are. If you wake up dead and realize you brought your Beast with you, the next locale will probably be no better than this one, and it could be worse.

You might as well make your stand against The Beast here, on the ground you know. You can win this battle here. You can head into the next realm feeling unfuckwithable, not whipped! That's why I wrote this book for you, my friend, so you could exit ultimately with great personal power.

If *The Seven* failed to help you, perhaps you read through this book too quickly, without stopping where advised to practice each hack, in sequence, before moving on to subsequent hacks? If so, there's still hope! Please review the list of questions above and see where you must refocus to unleash *The Seven*.

Most likely, your Beast is still devouring your life force, and it must be throttled. Shitty thoughts of self-pity, self-loathing, and suicide are being served up by The Beast, and must not be tolerated. Every time The Beast insists you'd be better off dead, tell it to fuck off and die! Then get on with *your life*.

If you are still feeling suicidal, I urge you to call The National Suicide Prevention Lifeline at 1-800-273-8255 right now.

Closer to Neutral

Okay, maybe you're not at Disneyland, but you have decided to hang around with us in the foam pit. Hopefully, *The Seven* has delivered palpable relief, and your emotional set point is at least closer to Neutral, as I promised. You're not exactly *happy*, but you're no longer miserable—and that's pretty terrific. And you did it without processing any issues!

If so, what now? Should you just consolidate your gains by continuing to practice *The Seven*, or should you expand your skills by investigating new alternatives, of which there are many? In essence, you are asking yourself The Question about your current emotional set point.

You now have sufficient life force running through you to support attempts at mindfulness and/or some form of cognitive therapy. Your efforts could boost your emotional set point safely into positive territory. There is little, if any, downside. I will list a few interesting and potentially useful books on these topics in the bibliography.

Perhaps you also want to connect more with the activities of life and with other people. You've pulled the metaphorical covers off your head and jumped out of bed, and you're eager to embrace the folly of your fellow man—a highly encouraging sign your depression and anxiety is dissipating.

With whom or what will you connect? Whether you join your local Freemason lodge, sign up for the PTA bowling league, join a hip hop dance team, or chant along with your town's Hare Krishnas, I encourage you to be sure your life force is enhanced by your participation.

You might even be ready to consider community service. If so, search online for "volunteer opportunities" for your local city, or try volunteermatch.org, helpvolunteer.app, catchafire.org, or thedeed.app to match your interests and skills with an ideal opportunity. You'll be glad you did. To quote author John Holmes, "There is no exercise better for the heart than reaching down and lifting people up."

At a minimum, consider signing up for a class or two on topics that interest you at your local community center or college. My simple suggestion is to gradually increase your participation in organized activities that spark your interest and boost your flow of life force. After all, an idle mind is The Beast's workshop.

What's Love Got to Do with It?

Perhaps you wonder how we've gotten this far without talking about love. Isn't manifesting love for ourselves, others, and our God the true purpose of life? How can one banish depression without love? As Oliver Wendell Holmes reportedly said, "Love is the master key that opens the gates of happiness."

I omitted love for three reasons. First, love resides on the opposite end of the emotional scale from depression. It's right up there at the very top, next to joy. I did not talk about joy, either, because it's impossible to leap sustainably from one end of the emotional scale to the other. Instead, we first strove to shift your emotional state from depression to anger, which is a more attainable step in the right direction. It's a small, big step!

Second, as you know from experience, you cannot generate loving feelings when The Beast is bombarding you with shitty thoughts. If I asked you to originate loving thoughts, and you failed miserably, you'd feel even worse, right? All I dared ask was for you to find a wisp of appreciation in those brief moments of silence won by your incessant bitch-slapping.

Third, the whole love thing is well beyond my pay grade. I don't know how to achieve it on demand, let alone advise you about it. Our culture confuses love with feelings of attraction and need, both of which can lead to disappointment and broken hearts. Unconditional love is not possessive and asks for nothing in return. Enduring unconditional love is a state of being, achieved after lifetime(s) of learning. It's certainly not a fast-acting antidote to depression and anxiety.

However, your emotional set point is now closer to Neutral, so you might want to explore the topic of love. Countless books and workshops can advise you. You can tackle the topic directly with the first book in the *Earth Life Series* by Sanaya Roman, *Living with Joy: Keys to Personal Power and Spiritual Transformation*.

Happy Trails

To each of you who has journeyed this far with me, I extend to you my heartfelt admiration and appreciation. I considered myself quixotic and even idiotic for writing a book for people who were too depressed even to begin it, let alone finish it. Yet, here we are!

I sincerely hope *The Seven* continues to help you to beat back The Beast and withstand the Mayhem of the Misfits, while finding a measure of fun in your daily life. You are the unfuckwithable boss of you. May your life force dazzle and your set point surge!

Bibliography

Where Do Thoughts Come From?

Gazzaniga, Michael S. *Consciousness Instinct: Unraveling the Mystery of How the Brain Makes the Mind.* Place of publication not identified: Farrar, Straus & Giroux, 2019. A comprehensive overview of scientific efforts to uncover how the brain creates consciousness.

Frey-Rohn, Liliane. *From Freud to Jung: a Comparative Study of the Psychology of the Unconscious.* Boston: Shambhala, 1990.

Schwartz, Richard C. *You Are the One You've Been Waiting For: Bringing Courageous Love to Intimate Relationships.* Oak Park, IL: Trailheads, 2008. IFS Family Systems Model (IFS) Dr. Schwartz developed his innovative IFS therapy that views individual consciousness as "an ecology of relatively discrete minds."

Unterman, Debbie. *Talking to My Selves: Learning to Love the Voices in Your Head.* Charleston, SC: Booksurge.com, 2009. Ms. Unternam advanced Dr. Quigley's Conference Room Therapy to include Inner Voice Integration of a person's 24 subpersonalities.

Monroe, Robert A. *Far Journeys.* New York: Harmony Books, 2016. The second of Monroe's three groundbreaking chronicles of his out-of-body travel.

Ruiz, Miguel. *The Four Agreements: A Practical Guide to Personal Freedom.* San Rafael, CA: Amber-Allen, 2017. Elegant and poetic prose on the Toltec approach to gaining personal freedom.

Castaneda, Carlos. *The Active Side of Infinity.* London: Harper Perennial, 2000. A fascinating recapitulation of the essential lessons of his apprenticeship with the Toltec sorcerer Don Juan.

Burns, David D. *Feeling Good.* New York: William Morrow, 2002. One of the most popular and bestselling books on Cognitive Behavioral Therapy.

Hicks, Esther, and Jerry Hicks. *Ask and It is Given: Learning to Manifest Your Desires.* New Delhi, India: Hay House Publications (India) Pvt. Ltd., 2017. Esther Hicks has gained a huge following channeling the entity Abraham, who promotes the Law of Attraction as the pathway to creating abundance.

Why Are We Here?

Carey, Ken. *The Starseed Transmissions.* San Francisco: HarperSanFrancisco, 1995. Originally published in 1982, this early classic of channeled, intuitive knowledge presents a startling new view of human evolution.

Roberts, Jane, and Robert F. Butts. *Seth Speaks: The Eternal Validity of the Soul.* San Rafael, CA: Amber-Allen Publ., 1994. Originally published in 1972, this channeled material from a discarnate entity named Seth became a cornerstone of the New Age movement in the 1980s.

Moen, Bruce. *Voyages into the Afterlife: Charting Unknown Territory.* Charlottesville, VA: Hampton Roads Pub., 1999. A protégé of

Robert Monroe, Moen wrote four books chronicling his vivid trance experiences in the after death environs.

Buhlman, William L. *The Secret of the Soul: Using Out-of-Body Experiences to Understand Our True Nature.* New York: HarperOne, 2011. The second book by this well-known out-of-body traveler and teacher.

Kolbert, Elizabeth. *The Sixth Extinction: An Unnatural History.* London etc.: Bloomsbury, 2015. The human species is the villain in the Pulitzer Prize-winning chronicle of the current mass extinction.

Walsch, Neale Donald. *Conversations with God: An Uncommon Dialogue.* Charlottesville, VA: Hampton Roads, 2014. An amazing three-part Q&A session between the author and God.

Castaneda, Carlos. *Journey to Ixtlan: The Lessons of Don Juan.* London: Bodley Head, 1991. The third entry into this series of eleven books. An excellent starting point for new readers, as it revisits the author's experiences in the first two books.

Lakhiani, Vishen. *The Code of the Extraordinary Mind: 10 Unconventional Laws to Redefine Your Life and Succeed On Your Own Terms.* New York: Rodale, 2016. An engaging primer on experts' techniques for becoming unfuckwithable.

The Daily Grind and CBO

Tolle, Eckhart. *A New Earth: Awakening to your life's purpose.* UK: Penguin Books, 2016. A more recent offering from the beloved author of the spiritual bestseller *The Power of Now.*

Covey, Stephen R. *The 7 Habits of Highly Effective People*. Provo, UT: Franklin Covey, 1998. A classic of personal development advice.

Ilardi, Stephen S. *The Depression Cure: The 6-Step Program to Beat Depression without Drugs*. Cambridge, MA: Da Capo Lifelong, 2010. A highly approachable prescription for overcoming depression through Therapeutic Lifestyle Change.

Gendlin, Eugene T. *Focusing*. New York, NY: Bantam, 2012. A short, powerful primer on relieving psychological distress.

Other Readings

Gyoerkoe, Kevin L., and Pamela S. Wiegartz. *10 Simple Solutions to Worry: How to Calm Your Mind, Relax Your Body, and Reclaim Your Life*. Oakland, CA: New Harbinger Publications, 2006. An easy approach to reducing anxiety and worry.

Huffington, Arianna Stassinopoulos. *Thrive: The Third Metric to Redefining Success and Creating a Life of Well-being, Wisdom, and Wonder*. London: WH Allen, 2015. A good directive for overly ambitious folks who are working too hard and sacrificing important aspects of life.

Block, Stanley H., and Carolyn Bryant. Block. *Come to Your Senses: Demystifying the Mind-body Connection*. New York: Atria Books, 2007. Promotes bridging and mind-body mapping to rest and heal the Identity System and access the True Self.

Bassett, Lucinda. *From Panic to Power: Proven Techniques to Calm Your Anxieties, Conquer Your Fears, and Put You in Control of Your*

Life. New York, NY: CollinsLiving, 2005. Straightforward advice on building personal power and confidence.

Amen, Daniel G., and Lisa C. Routh. *Healing Anxiety and Depression*. New York, NY: Berkley Books, 2004. Dr. Amen is a highly regarded psychiatrist and best-selling author who pioneered the concept of brain health to solve psychological problems. Includes comprehensive approaches to seven types of anxiety and depression.

Hari, Johann. *Lost Connections: Uncovering the Real Causes of Depression and the Unexpected Solutions*. Place of publication not identified: BLOOMSBURY, 2019. Engaging and well-researched overview of malaise in modern society, the limitations of medication, and the value of alternative approaches to overcoming depression.

About the Author

Michael McTeigue considers himself the quintessential disillusioned New Age idealist. As a young man, he enthusiastically embraced the great promise of the human potential movement and mankind's imminent spiritual awakening. When the dawn of the new millennium came and went and nothing much changed, Michael gradually descended into a dogged depression born of thwarted ambitions and broken dreams. He spent the ensuing years digging his way out. In the process, Michael developed *The Seven Life Hacks*, which he hopes will help lighten the load for each person who tries them. Michael has written four books. He is married with two daughters and resides in San Mateo, CA.

Contact Michael at The7LifeHacks@gmail.com.

About the Illustrator

Lawrence Moorcroft is a commercial artist, illustrator, and feature film animator. He has designed and built theme park rides and monsters in glass fiber. He enjoys drawing and illustrating books and children's stories. Lawrence recently turned to writing an adventure story for boys called The Other Marco. A blog of the same name illustrates and promotes this venture.

Made in the USA
Las Vegas, NV
24 January 2021

16454519R00105